PAPA'S LETTERS

Love via First-Class Male

Judith C. Lovell

authorHOUSE®

AuthorHouse™
1663 Liberty Drive
Bloomington, IN 47403
www.authorhouse.com
Phone: 1-800-839-8640

Published by AuthorHouse   05/07/2015

ISBN: 978-1-4772-9977-7 (sc)
ISBN: 978-1-4772-9976-0 (hc)
ISBN: 978-1-4772-9975-3 (e)

Library of Congress Control Number: 2012923644

Print information available on the last page.

This book is printed on acid-free paper.

This book is dedicated to the entire "Hurd Herd."

Family is Divine

"For you are all children of the light and of the day; we don't belong to darkness and night. So be on your guard, not asleep like the others. Stay alert and be clearheaded. Night is the time when people sleep and drinkers get drunk. But let us who live in the light be clearheaded, protected by the armor of faith and love, and wearing as our helmet the confidence of our salvation."

— 1 Thessalonians, chapter 5 verses 5 to 8.

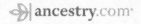

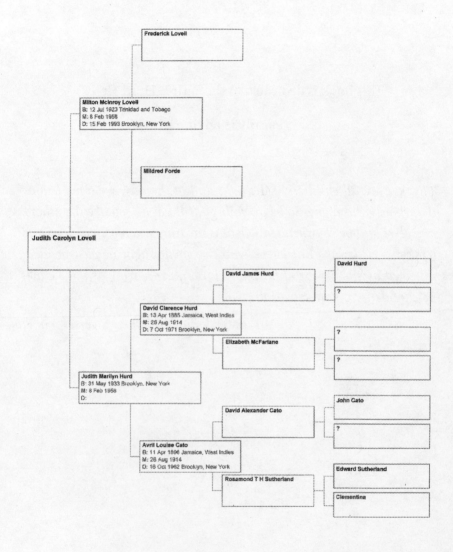

Frederick Lovell

Milton McInroy Lovell
B: 12 Jul 1923 Trinidad and Tobago
M: 8 Feb 1958
D: 15 Feb 1993 Brooklyn, New York

Mildred Forde

Judith Carolyn Lovell

David James Hurd

David Hurd

?

David Clarence Hurd
B: 13 Apr 1885 Jamaica, West Indies
M: 26 Aug 1914
D: 7 Oct 1971 Brooklyn, New York

Elizabeth McFarlane

?

?

Judith Marilyn Hurd
B: 31 May 1933 Brooklyn, New York
M: 8 Feb 1958
D:

David Alexander Cato

John Cato

?

Avril Louise Cato
B: 11 Apr 1896 Jamaica, West Indies
M: 26 Aug 1914
D: 16 Oct 1962 Brooklyn, New York

Rosamond T H Sutherland

Edward Sutherland

Clementina

Table of Contents

Introduction 1

1. Papa and the Old Country 7

2. Papa and the New Country. 35

3. Papa's Letters to Grandma 55

4. Papa and Grandma: Life after the Letters . . .111

5. This is Not the End 119

Notes 131

About the Author 135

Acknowledgments

My most sincere and humble thanks to the following people

For with God

Nothing will be Impossible ... Amen!

To Papa, David Clarence Hurd (deceased), and Grandma, Avril Louise Cato Hurd (deceased), for without you, we could not savor this delightful love story. Though I do not have all of the letters sent over a period of almost a year, I was able to do some research, including personal interviews, to piece together our amazing story.

To my mother, Judith Hurd Lovell, and father, Milton M. Lovell (deceased), for all of your emotional support and intellectual stimulation through the years; you provided the space for family get-togethers and festive celebrations after Grandma's death. It was during these valuable family occasions that I sat, riveted to my seat, listening and writing down the family history.

To my brother, David A. Lovell (deceased), for those extremely special times we shared together with Papa and Grandma. May you rest in peace.

To my children, Kwame C. Prescod and Ayanna E. Prescod, for your inspiration, motivation, and periodic literary critique and commentary. Remember, you are fruit of this magnificent tree. Do not ever forget your roots. Pass on our story to your children and your children's children.

To Aunt (Bobbie) Avril Hurd Latham (deceased), and Aunt Rosie, Rosemonde Hurd Rutledge (deceased). As you were Papa's first two children, I depended on you to remember names, dates, places, and events. You never disappointed me. Even during my childhood, you lovingly answered all my questions. You both kept the family history alive, exciting, and accurate.

To Aunt Annie, Ruth Andrea Hurd Foreman. As Papa's last child and the baby, twenty-four years younger than his first, you sometimes expressed an entirely different generational view. Thank you for your powerful and thoughtful introduction. You have shared your exquisite poetry and writings with the family, helping us to maintain a most important connection to the past through the creative arts.

To Uncle Jimmy, David J. Hurd, and Uncle Rodney, Rodney M. Hurd. As you were Papa's only sons, and ten years apart, your storytelling expressed the male point of view from two different eras and two different perspectives.

To Cousin Norma, **Norma E. Walters,** for being my primary contact in Jamaica. Your grandfather, Tom Hurd, and my grandfather, David Hurd, were brothers. As family, they looked out for each other. The letters indicate they lived together in New York with their new wives, beginning in 1914. Their wives, Mattie (Matilda) Cunningham Hurd and Avril Cato Hurd, were cousins; therefore we are related on both sides of the family. As a teacher, historian, and community advocate, you have helped me significantly to fill in the blanks in our family tree. You did so during numerous telephone conversations and several visits to your most welcoming home in Brown's Town, Saint Ann.

To Aunt Roslyn, Roslyn Cato Black (deceased), and Cousin Shirley, Shirley Mishore, mother and daughter born on the same date, December 23rd. As Grandma's baby sister, you passionately shared the Catos' legacy with me through the years. I simply enjoyed sitting down for hours at your table. While snacking on your delicious fish cakes and homemade ginger beer, I listened attentively to your animated storytelling of life in Jamaica. Cousin Shirley, after your mother died on her one hundredth birthday, you filled in the historical gaps for me.

To the *Carib News* for initially printing the four-part series "Papa's Letters" and circulating it nationally and internationally, using both hard copy and electronic format. As a result of the newspaper's wide distribution, many enthusiastic readers contacted me via email. They sent wonderful comments and asked question after question, inquiring further about Papa, Grandma, about the letters, the family, and my role as storyteller, which lead me to write my first book.

To all those who read the four-part series in the *Carib News* and enjoyed it, and to those who took the time to send comments or questions.

To Hakim Hasan. You encouraged me to print the four part-series and to write this subsequent book. As you say, your genius is the ability to pinpoint trends and identify key contacts. You have always helped me make the necessary professional contacts to promote my career. Through the years you have given me much support, constructive criticism, and sound advice.

To the countless number of people I have questioned, watched, and communicated with over the years to be able to tell this magnificent story.

Introduction

"Praise ye the Lord. Blessed is the man that feareth the Lord, that delighteth greatly in his commandments. His seed shall be mighty upon earth: the generation of the upright shall be blessed."

— Psalm 112, verses 1 and 2.

Papa…handsome, gentle, sweet, strong, dramatic, smart, charming, clever, thespian, engaging, rhythmic, magnificent, ministering…and on and on…

I don't remember how we got onto the subject, but I did ask Ma – more than once – how she met Papa and how they finally got together. I imagined it was some enchanted evening in a gorgeous Jamaican retreat – when she saw a stranger across a crowded room and somehow she knew she would see him again. Romantic emotions had taken hold of their senses stirring a stunning innocent teenager to fall madly in love with a mature handsome gentleman.

But no – I was almost disappointed when I discovered she and Papa had never met in person until the afternoon before they were married. Imagine that!

I never thought of planning a marriage to someone I had never laid eyes on, or to someone with whom I had never had a conversation. And thinking back to my own courtship, there was a meaningful kiss or three that led up to "yes" let's get married. Then, there were the parental announcements, getting permission and serious planning. But that's another story.

I don't remember exactly how I felt when I realized the truth about Ma and Papa, but I usually have a twinkle in my eye when I tell folks about my parents' exciting and unique courtship. But, I must admit that I never had the complete story you will have after reading this book and I certainly do not have the flair for its presentation.

As I reminisce about my parents, I consider with pride and wonder just how special they were, and are. I'm not the only one who thinks that "Momsie" and "Popsie," as I called them, were exceptional in so many ways, individually and together as a couple.

So many in our midst are living in multi-fractured families, sometimes I feel like our family is the odd one out. In my heart I still have the Biblical belief that God means marriage to be a lifelong engagement like the one my parents demonstrated.

Since I was the last of six siblings born to them in a marriage that lasted 48 years, I would like to think my parents were ahead of these times. Since so many couples in the 21st Century are meeting through online dating with long distance telephone texting correspondence, it may have been just another wrinkle in the universe. We've read and heard about mail-order brides in many places like America's early western development. Some of those couples were destined for successful partnerships and strong family heritage, even though their match making was often based only on convenience.

The thing about Momsie and Popsie is each one was seeking the perfect mate for a lifetime relationship built on love, caring, mutual respect and spiritual guidance. They had a real courtship on paper, which to me made it even more binding and truly awesome. It had the element of distance. It had the intrigue of complete strangers reaching out to create a brand new lifetime of support for love in married life built primarily on faith. It also had the ring of truth; their roots were culturally and spiritually intertwined and compatible. And if that were not enough, they were both born in beautiful historic Jamaica, West Indies – whose motto is, "Out of Many, One People."

> African; Jamaican; America "Me."
> The fruit that fell far from the tree
> The product of unique complexity
> Proudly acknowledges nativity.

I wonder if young people today care much about roots for a cultural and spiritual compatibility. Many are excited by the span of outreach that widens the availability of partners using the internet to broaden individual interests, capabilities and choices.

But, back to our family; Popsie and I began a very special camaraderie when I was about five years old. I was in kindergarten one day when all the children were sent to the auditorium. Each child in turn was called to sit on a stool under a purple ultraviolet light. When it was my turn, I had to unbraid my hair. I nervously sat on the stool while a stranger searched through my hair with a couple of cold metal tongue depressors. When she finished, I was segregated from my class. Alone, I waited for my sister. She would take me home.

My sister Judith Marilyn was in 6th grade at the same school. She took me home with a note to my parents. Later I found out the school's health team was checking students for ringworm and apparently I had tested positive. I was assigned to go to a clinic for treatments which included shaving my head. Popsie decided to protect his little girl from further hurt and shame. He cut off all my hair himself; and as my hair fell to the floor, I felt his tear drops fall onto my scalp. I was as bald as a marble for the next six months.

Momsie had this great idea. She braided the hair Popsie had detached from my scalp. She attached the two braids to a bonnet as a disguise for my unfeminine, unattractive, bald, toothless condition. She, however, underestimated the craftiness of my five year old classmates. They were clever and mean. I ignored them for the most part until they couldn't stand the mystery under the bonnet any longer.

One day, on the way to the girls' toilet room, a group of girls caught me, threw me down on the cement floor and yanked off my bonnet. They squealed with excitement as they tossed the bonnet with the dangling, lifeless braids pinned inside, back and forth between them. They taunted me for trying to fool them; for having the nerve to come to school with a bald head and phony braids. A teacher found me. She brought me to the principal's office and called my parents. A few minutes later my strong Popsie showed up and rescued me. He was determined to shield his little girl from more ridicule; he kept me out of school for the entire semester.

As it turned out, I never had ringworm. I had had a false diagnosis but stayed out of school for the rest of the term. I got to know and fall in love with my Popsie. Being last of six siblings was like being at the bottom of the food chain. Popsie now became my champion, my protector, my almost constant companion, during those days when I was the joke at every family gathering while I stayed home from school.

You may not believe it but the best film of all time for me was playing in theaters while I was hanging out with Popsie. "The Wizard of Oz" was the film I saw in stunning color. We saw lots of movies together during that school term. It cost about 15 cents for me and a few cents more for Popsie to get into the theatre. He never tired of having me with him. I was his last "pickney," his baby. And though he had a wife, other children, work and responsibilities, he made time for me. I felt very special and cherished.

He gave me my first lessons in banking at the Dime Savings Bank. He let me carry the deposit slips with cash up to the teller and wait for the entry in the savings account book. Though I was kept out of school, Popsie personally schooled me every day. He taught me life-lessons I could have never learned in school.

On Saturdays at home, we all prepared the Bible readings for Sunday. Popsie was the Lay Reader at St. Philip's Church in Brooklyn. He read the lessons at church during the worship service. But we at home were given the full dramatic presentation of the scriptures as he passionately rehearsed his assigned readings.

I felt pretty much grown up by the time I realized my parents originated from this whole other country. Oddly enough, though I have traveled to several Caribbean Islands, I have never visited my parents' birth-homeland. I have never felt home sick about it. Although, I do hope I may have the chance to visit my home away from home someday. I realized my parents were very comfortable with their native ancestry and with life in their adopted country.

I have always identified with their complete acceptance of dual nationality. Still, only three of my siblings actually lived in Jamaica as children spending most of their lives in New York City. Later generations have branched out only a little to include Canada, North Carolina and Maryland.

But no one, since Popsie and Momsie, has been brave enough or adventurous enough to plan to successfully raise a family in a completely new and different country and culture.

It was a privilege to actually experience a complete and wholesome second-generation family. My father loved me for 32 years of my life and has remained alive and well in my thoughts and prayers even unto this very moment. I only had my Mom for 23 years and of course they were the best years because I had both parents at the same time.

Momsie died in 1962 and my sister Judith Marilyn took possession of the collection of keepsake letters. I was intrigued by their actual existence. I had heard about them throughout my lifetime but I assumed they had been lost down through the years of growing, moving, and discarding things. She let me read them. I pored over them and devoured them sometimes with gales of laughter or pensive wonder, tiny tears and sheer amazement. I treasured them and hoped to publish them "some day."

Some years later, as I was gathering my belongings to move into what became my permanent family residence, I came across the letters again. I eagerly consumed them again and decided to pass them on.

We never located Momsie's letters to Popsie and yet I have a vivid recollection of a letter that was address to "My Dearest Mr. Hurd." The letters did exist and were the inspiration of many of Popsie's replies. I still fantasize about reading all the letters as a complete, historical narrative and basking in the warmth of their love again and again.

Besides being family, the author and I share an unusually close relationship based on our appreciation for the written word, especially when words are expressed in a delightful rhythm of phrases and verses. But mostly, we share affection for the man she called "Papa;" the man who wrote to her Grandma. I gave Papa's letter to my niece Judith Carolyn in the hope she would fulfill my latent dream to share his awe-inspiring love letters with the community-at-large and then maybe with the entire world.

Thankfully, this volume is her labor of love and legacy.

Ruth Andrea Hurd Foreman

Sixth and Last Child of David C. and Avril L. Hurd

December 13, 2010

CHAPTER 1
Papa and the Old Country

So he sent, and brought him in. Now he was ruddy, with bright eyes, and good looking. And the Lord said, "Arise, anoint him; for this is the one!"

— 1 Samuel, chapter 16 verse 12.

(Map of Jamaica – with National Heroes)

About ten years ago, I inherited a bundle of love letters and diary notes written by my maternal grandfather, David Clarence Hurd. He composed these writings while living in Brooklyn, New York. Papa, as my grandfather was lovingly called, was born in Brown's Town, Saint Ann, Jamaica, West Indies, on April 13, 1885. Beginning in October of 1913, he wrote to Avril Louise Cato, who lived in Port Antonio, Jamaica. Initially pen pals, they wrote to each other for nearly a year. The pen pal phenomenon was quite popular back then. Customarily, through letter writing a pen pal connected with another to learn about his country, customs, and lifestyle. Some pen pal relationships, like that of my future grandparents, blossomed into blissful romance.

David got to know his future bride through letter writing. After forming a loving bond built on trust and faith, he poured out his heart to her. He sent many impassioned love letters. He proposed marriage in a letter. She accepted the proposal in a letter. They physically met each other for the first time on Tuesday, August 25, 1914, in Port Antonio, the day before their wedding ceremony.

Papa's love letters are characterized by a keen sense of novelistic detail. They are a record of my grandfather's courtship of my grandmother and his observations as a Jamaican immigrant living in Brooklyn during the very beginning of the twentieth century. After reading and digesting the collection of writings, I realized that besides building a strong, loving relationship with his future beloved wife, he meticulously set the stage for her smooth transition to America with his letters.

He informed Grandma about the United States with deep thought and insight. Papa enlightened her on a social, cultural, and historical level, possibly circumventing the culture shock he himself had painfully experienced when he arrived. I inherited only some of Papa's letters and none of Grandma's letters. I know many more existed, because my mother and aunts remember reading all of Papa's letters and Grandma's responses. Sadly, through the years, letters were somehow lost. Some of the story had to be carefully pieced together with research, an undertaking I enjoyed tremendously. The rest of our story I leave to your imagination.

I grew up with Papa and with my parents in a strict, religious Caribbean home in Crown Heights, Brooklyn. It is no accident we thrived in that area. Caribbean people have been flocking to that neighborhood and buying homes since the 1920s. Crown Heights is centrally located, and the IRT (Interborough Rapid Transit) subway along Eastern Parkway and the IND (Independent) subway train lines are easily accessible. Caribbean commuters traveled to and from Harlem, downtown Brooklyn, and other areas of New York City frequently and easily.[1] They settled in Crown Heights, opened businesses and restaurants, and established an amazing network, creating a Caribbean home away from home.

And of course, every summer, during the Labor Day weekend, Caribbean people from all over the world come together in Crown Heights to "play mas" (to join in the masquerade) and reconnect with loved ones at home and abroad. Since my childhood, The West Indian-American Day Carnival Association has organized the parade of elaborate customs, colorful and creative costumes, and calypso and reggae bands. My family, Papa, and I did not have far to travel to join in the carnival celebrations. We lived only a block and a half away from the parade route along Eastern Parkway.

During the nine years I lived with my Papa, I got to know him well. On the other hand, I was only three years old when Grandma died. I do have memories of walking down Eastern Parkway's prodigious treelined sidewalks hand in hand with her, feeding the birds. I remember the excitement felt each time Grandma came to visit. My younger brother and only sibling David Alexander and I screamed hysterically, "Granny's here, Granny's here," upon spotting her at the window. We would run and usually hide inside the bathroom.

Once she had entered the living room with mommy, we dashed out of hiding, screaming, "Surprise! Surprise!" We would then run into her humongous, powerfully strong arms with their long, regal fingers and stunningly perfect nails.

(Christmas 1960 in my mother's living room - Grandma is holding my brother David and I am standing patiently very nearby)

Grandma was a natural beauty with a flawlessly chiseled little nose, dainty mouth, and a long gazelle-like neck. Her soft gray hair was usually pulled away from her face. At home, Grandma usually wore a housecoat, and her well-endowed bosom comforted all twelve grandchildren, at one time or another.

When she added a tinge of makeup and styled herself for church or a social event with Papa, Grandma transformed from naturally beautiful to strikingly gorgeous.

(At Grandma's house - in her arms are my brother David Alexander,
cousin Rodney Hurd, (four of Uncle Rodney's five children) left to right
on floor cousins Patricia Hurd, Robin Hurd, Me, cousin Sherry Hurd,
Aunt Cecile Hurd (Uncle Jimmy's wife) with their daughter cousin
Leslie Hurd in her arms, and Aunt Rosie seated in the next room.)

I also remember how Grandma and Papa opened their home and
heart to the entire "Hurd Herd" and their friends every Wednesday
evening for supper. The most scrumptious aromas and meals sailed
out of Grandma's kitchen. On a Wednesday night, my mother and
aunts could be found busily helping Grandma with the cooking.
While creating magic with utensils, they chatted about almost
everything: whose child was the most amazing, the latest fashions,
workplace challenges, and their most heartfelt topic—their men. As
a toddler, I did not understand everything they were saying; however,
those same discussions continued through the years every time we
got together.

(Grandma posing after services at St. Philip's Episcopal
Church on Decatur Street in Brooklyn. Papa and Grandma
loved their church home and brought several family members
and friends there to worship over the decades.)

In the dining room, the men heatedly debated with pounding fists,
dramatized words, and exaggerated expressions their three most
favorite topics: race, religion, and politics. It was the 1960s, and those

were turbulent times in America. Minister Malcolm X, Reverend Dr. Martin Luther King, Jr., President John F. Kennedy, his brother Bobby, and various civil rights activists were constantly in the news. The men of the family always had new questions to argue about before, during, and after Wednesday night dinner. These intellectually passionate exchanges and zealous discussions still inspire me today, for the younger generation of cousins has taken up right where the elders left off.

In the living room, the children, mostly cousins, played games with each other. We played different games: tag—you're it; red light, green light, one, two, three; and hide and go seek. Though we were often chastised for being too noisy or too playful, we had lots of fun together. Usually children in my family were forbidden to listen to, much less join in adult conversation. However, I spent most of my time with the adults. I do not know why they allowed me to listen to their private conversations, but they did. I simply conjecture that maybe it was because I exuded an older spirit, or maybe the elders instinctively knew I was the "chosen one" to keep the family history alive. In any case, I would usually settle into an inconspicuous corner and listen quietly as my Papa, parents, uncles, and aunts told stories. I observed everything and made mental notes. Even as a child, I found family history fascinating.

Those days it seemed as if every time we met there was a new addition to the family or a new reason for celebration. It was always festive and joyful. Grandma's house and heart were enormous. There was enough room, nourishment, and love for everyone. She spent most of her time shopping, cooking, washing, and cleaning for her beloved family. Grandma devoted her life to us and worked tirelessly, and I mean tirelessly, making sure all of our needs were met.

During Grandma's last days on Earth, my mother regularly carted my brother and me to see her. Grandma was extremely weak, in a lot of pain, and spent most of her time in bed. My mother remembered that, in empathy, if Grandma limped, so did I. If Grandma moaned, so did I. If Grandma felt pain, I said I felt pain. Surprisingly, with all of the recollections I do have of my formative years, I do not remember any of that. I must have suppressed those memories. As some psychologists suggest, we may repress memories of traumatic experiences because they are much too difficult to bear.

Whereas I have no recollection of Grandma's pain, my cousin David Hurd (the son of Papa's first son, David James Hurd, also known as Uncle Jimmy) remembers Grandma's pain intensely. Nine years my senior, David recalls that during her final year, Grandma frequently cried out from the excruciating pain, "O Master, let me walk with Thee." This poem turned hymn, with words written by Reverend Washington Gladden, is found in the 1982 hymnal, used by Episcopalians today. The first two verses declare:

O Master, let me walk with Thee
in lowly paths of service free;
tell me Thy secret, help me bear
the strain of toil, the fret of care.

Help me the slow of heart to move
by some clear, winning word of love,
teach me the wayward feet to stay,
and guide them in the homeward way."

As a young boy, David said he felt extremely helpless and quite distraught, seeing the family matriarch in such distress and possibly asking God to end it all.

The memories I do have of Grandma I fervently cling to; memories of Grandma and Wednesday night supper and times with her and with my brother and feeding the birds along the parkway. I often muse over those moments, because they were overwhelmingly precious. I feel blessed to have experienced the love of both maternal grandparents, even though it was only for a short period of time.

Grandma was sixty-six years of age when she died on Tuesday, October 16, 1962. It was a date to remember, for on that gloomy day, the Cuban Missile Crisis began; there was talk of possible nuclear attacks. My beloved Grandma had left me and almost immediately, the world had become a scary place. My Papa was seventy-seven when Grandma passed. His soul mate and beloved wife of forty-eight years had left him much too soon.

At first he was in denial about Grandma's death. After that, he seemed dreadfully despondent and lost. He said their house on Union Street was enormous, lonely, and cold without her. Grandma's death was devastating to my mother, as well. Mommy and Grandma had been so very close through the years. Mommy thought having Papa live with her would undoubtedly help ease the pain for both of them.

So after selling his own house, just a couple blocks away, he moved in with us on Lincoln Place. With Papa there, our house instantly became the new official meeting ground for family members and their friends. Mommy did not continue the Wednesday night dinners. However, she painstakingly prepared provisions for a full house during major holidays like Thanksgiving and Christmas and important celebrations like Papa's birthday. I particularly loved those festive gatherings, for animated storytelling filled the air of the dining room. My daddy, Milton McInroy Lovell, an immigrant from Port of Spain, Trinidad, truly enjoyed having his adopted family at the house. Many of his own biological family members were far away, dispersed around the world.

Daddy, one of Papa's three sons-in-law, deeply respected, admired, and loved his extraordinary father through marriage. Though he was no pushover and owned the house Papa now resided in, it was Papa who presided as patriarch supreme from the top floor apartment of our brownstone. He paid Daddy rent each month and would not have it any other way. Papa lived with us for nine incredible years before reuniting with his beloved wife and partner, Avril. I got to know my grandfather really well while living with him. I adored him.

Papa was true to his astrological sign of Aries, the first sign of the zodiac. Arian personalities are known for their leadership qualities. He was strong, bold, brave, creative, confident, energetic, opinionated, and charming. Once he gave an order, most sane folk obeyed immediately. He was a mover and shaker who loved a challenge.

I remember a confrontation involving Papa as if it were yesterday. About eleven years old, I had just come home from St. Gregory the Great Roman Catholic Elementary School on St. John's Place. I quickly jumped out of my uniform and anxiously turned on the television, not wanting to miss a minute of my favorite soap opera. Our television sat majestically in front of the living room window. The blinds were wide open while the sun shone brightly inside. To my horror, I observed a tall, husky man wearing a long dark trench coat and knitted skullcap, using a sizable crowbar. The man was inconspicuously prying open Aunt Rosie's front door.

Aunt Rosie (Rosemonde Hurd Rutledge) was one of Papa's six children. Papa and Grandma had four girls and two boys. Papa always referred to his two sets of children. He had two girls and boy, Avril (Bobbie), Rosemonde (Rosie), and David (Jimmy); then, ten years later, he had a boy and two girls, Rodney, Judith, and Ruth Andrea (Annie). Rosemonde was his second child and my second mother. Aunt Rosie owned the brownstone directly across the street from ours. In fact, it was Papa who had learned of the pending sale of that house and had skillfully negotiated the deal for his daughter.

Papa loved having his family close by and adroitly maneuvered to surround himself with kin. So after Aunt Rosie bought the house, she rented the top floor apartment to Ruth Andrea (Aunt Annie), her baby sister. Aunt Annie lived there with her husband, William Foreman (Uncle Billy), and son Christopher (Cousin Chris). The family's property was under attack that day. Without hesitation, I yelled upstairs for my Papa. He answered me. Thank God he was home, I thought. I hurriedly ran up the stairs and in between breaths told Papa exactly what was happening.

Without delay, he grabbed his gold-headed walking stick and determinedly prepared to defend us. Papa was about 5 feet 10 inches tall with a slim but sturdy build. Red undertones added warmth to his cappuccino-colored complexion, and brilliant blue highlights radiated from each pupil, accentuating his gorgeous gray eyes. That day he wore a suit with a handsome vest—a vest, I might add, he designed and constructed himself. Even under duress, Papa remained dapper.

(My Dapper Papa)

This David, a son of David, a highly favored anointed man of God, intended to confront that brazen burglar singlehandedly. Now home alone, I stayed inside and watched the adventure through the window at first. My parents and the rest of the family were all still at work. It was only about two o'clock in the afternoon. I never once thought to call the police. Why should I? My Papa could handle anything. He was a superman.

In less than five minutes, the thief appeared from inside the house, apparently disorientated. He looked as if he had seen a *duppy* (Jamaican patois for a ghost). As the bandit frequently glanced over his shoulder and tried to get out of Papa's way, he desperately clutched a big, black, bulky bag. He scurried down the outside steps onto the sidewalk with Papa in hot pursuit. The young intruder hurriedly ran down the block, purposefully dropping stolen items onto the street. Now outside, I saw a gigantic red plastic piggy bank, heavy with coins, crash onto the sidewalk and crack open.

I believe the thief threw away some of the goods to make his getaway easier and faster. Papa yelled, "Thief! Thief!" louder and louder as he ran, waving his cane high in the air. Alerted neighbors began to appear outside on their stoops. A rather rotund Good Samaritan tried to stop the criminal from turning the corner. With one powerful shove, the bandit thrust the neighbor to the ground. That evil burglar never once touched my grandfather. The chase continued for about another block.

Papa never did catch the burglar, but he did recover most of the stolen items. Cousin Chris's bank, filled with what seemed to have been thousands of pennies, and Uncle Billy's, much-loved professional camera and its attachments, were safe. Papa, my hero, was eighty-five years old at the time. Bible studies instructor, Reverend Rita Story of St. Paul Community Baptist Church, where Reverend David Brawley is Senior Pastor, would say, "That man had dominion over things above him, things below him, and things around him." Papa did not allow his physical environment to control him.

He daily deepened his spiritual bond with his Creator: praying unwaveringly, mediating faithfully, and reading his Bible religiously. Throughout his life, Papa remained deeply rooted in the word of God. He fearlessly ventured into the unknown while carefully listening to the voice of the Lord. "This is my command—be strong and courageous! Do not be afraid or discouraged. For the Lord your God is with you wherever you go" (Joshua 1:9). Hallelujah, I will never ever forget that remarkable day!

Papa was also brilliant, compelling, and theatrical; a natural griot. In West Africa, the land of the ancestors, a griot is a historian, poet, and master storyteller. Wow! After hearing Papa's stories, one remained awestruck. I especially loved when Papa dramatized life in Jamaica. I strongly agree with him: God abundantly endowed his third largest island in the Caribbean.

I traveled to Jamaica for the first time in the summer of 1982. I was a Brooklyn College undergraduate with a dual major in sociology and urban planning and a minor in African studies. I eagerly enrolled in the college's summer course, "Seminar in Jamaica." Brooklyn College students who enrolled in the seminar would travel together to Jamaica; attend classes; and conduct research there. I registered for that course for three main reasons: to step foot on the land of my grandparent's birth and personally experience Jamaica; to continue my research on the status of working-class women in the world; and to fulfill my requirement for my bachelor of arts degree.

Professor Cuthbert Thomas, the seminar's coordinator, the class, and I roomed and studied at the University of the West Indies at Mona, located in the parish of Saint Andrew. Professors at Mona designed, developed, and implemented a rigorous schedule of classes for us, focused on the sociopolitical environment of Jamaica. I delved right away into my research topic: the economic condition of working-class women in Jamaica.

At the time, Edward Seaga, a member of the Jamaica Labor Party (JLP) was prime minister. Seaga a Bostonian and a Harvard graduate was born to Jamaican parents. His platform included strengthening ties with the United States and breaking them with Cuba. Republican Ronald Reagan was president of the United States. Margaret Thatcher, a Conservative, served as the United Kingdom's first female prime minister. Jamaica had acquired independence from Britain in August of 1962, and the overall presence of women in the workplace had steadily increased since the 1970s.[2] According to my research in 1982, I found the presence of women in the workplace had increased mainly in the traditionally held female positions: nurses, teachers, and caregivers. The glass ceiling remained a barrier for professional women aspiring to be successful executives and influential leaders.

It was during this first visit that I spent quality time in Brown's Town with a prominent Jamaican woman, my cousin Norma Walters. Norma is the granddaughter of Tom Hurd, Papa's eldest brother. She is a respected justice of the peace, historian, teacher, musical director, and singer. Norma took me all around Brown's Town and introduced me to relatives I had never met. I visited Brown's Town Tabernacle Church, where Papa worshipped and where his father, my great-grandfather, had preached.

(Brown's Town Tabernacle Church)

I stepped foot on the old homestead where Papa and his siblings grew up. I saw the approximate place on the property where Papa's parents, my great-grandfather and great-grandmother, are buried.

(My great-grandparents are buried on the land at the old homestead – Standfast, Brown's Town, St. Ann)

The old folks died in 1932, approximately a week apart. My great-grandfather was ninety-seven years old and my great-grandmother was ninety-six. Relatives in Brown's Town told me that my great-grandfather had been sick for months and had succumbed to his illness. During the burial ceremonies, my great-grandmother, afflicted with dementia, finally realized it was her beloved husband who had passed. She stopped speaking, and within days made her own transition. I learned so much and thoroughly enjoyed my visit to Brown's Town. The stay was much too short, though. I could only spend a weekend with Cousin Norma, because I had to return to the university for Monday morning classes. I vowed to return to the old homestead someday.

During another one of my weekend excursions away from the university, I experienced Reggae Sunsplash. Reggae Sunsplash, the forerunner to today's Reggae SunFest, was an annual outdoor cultural extravaganza, held in Jarrett Park, Montego Bay. Sunsplash was originally created to encourage tourism during the summer. Numerous artists performed onstage, and the audience packed the park for hours of merriment. That year, Yellowman was the highlighted reggae star. In the sweltering August heat, I, along with thousands of other revelers, enthusiastically sang and danced to the music. As Bob Marley said, we were "one love, one heart." And we got together and felt alright, enjoying some Jamaican culture.

After an exciting but exhausting weekend of festivities in Jarrett Park, I planned a more relaxing venture for the following weekend. Some classmates and I drove to the parish of Saint Thomas to experience the famous therapeutic mineral baths. As we leisurely toured the island from Kingston to Morant Bay, I witnessed for the first time heart-wrenching poverty of shantytowns. These scattered, improvised slum areas provided few solutions to the basic human needs for shelter, water, safety, and esteem. Shocked by the contrast with the extreme opulence and affluence I had experienced in Jamaica's wealthy Beverly Hills suburbs, I remained in a state of disbelief as we drove.

We stopped in Morant Bay, the capital of Saint Thomas, for lunch. I found the people friendly, the city vibrant, and the place rich with history. I was told by residents that extreme poverty, rampant racism, and high unemployment had ignited a burning desire in the masses for immediate equality in 1865. People were suffering. Paul Bogle, a Baptist deacon and activist, led numerous black men and women in a protest for justice. In unison, they forcefully marched to the courthouse on October 11th. And after being shot at by unsympathetic authorities, Bogle and his followers set the courthouse afire. Papa often spoke about the Morant Bay Rebellion. On my visit, I saw a statue of national hero Bogle, erected in 1965, which stood prominently in front of the courthouse.

We walked around sightseeing for awhile in Morant Bay, and then settled down for some lunch. I enjoyed a Jamaican specialty, jerk chicken. From what the chef told me, jerk refers to the style of cooking. He greeted us by saying, *"Irie"* [a traditional greeting]. "Yeah mon, I&I [the communal I] rubb down da deaders [season the meat] good in ital spices them—cook it in da pit fire in da yard." "Ital food dat [ital or vital food is natural, wholesome food without additives or preservatives] yeah mon." We hungrily waited about an hour before our food was served, but it was well worth the wait. The chicken was succulent, hot, and seasoned through to the bone. We *nyamed* down the food [ate heartily]. The chef smiled and said, "I-Man mash it up fi dem." In other words, his meal was a huge success. Yeah mon! The modern way of cooking jerk is in the oven. But I must say the taste of that scrumptious chicken was so amazingly delicious that I now prefer my jerk cooked in an open fire pit like that one.

Once we finished our lunch, we headed to Bath Mineral Springs. According to legend, a slave on the run discovered these miracle waters. After soaking himself, he realized his persistent illness had been cured; the open sores on his legs were gone. People have been seeking out these healing waters ever since. At the time of my visit to the baths, I was in my early twenties and in fantastic shape and perfect health. Out of curiosity, I wanted to experience the hot baths. The waters there are rich in sulfate, lime, and salts and are excellent for ailments like arthritis.[3] The bath relaxed my entire being. As I soaked in the luxuriously warm water, rich in minerals, I vowed to come back to Saint Thomas for a longer stay, someday.

Back on campus, some of my classmates and I often swam in the sea very early in the morning. The water was always clean, warm, and inviting. Invigorated, we would then shower, eat breakfast, and head to class. Our designated classroom was a small lecture hall. I usually sat in the front, not wanting to miss a word of those scintillating discussions.

On one occasion at Mona, we experienced a real treat. The National Dance Theatre Company of Jamaica (NDTC) performed, under the direction of its founder, creative genius Ralston Milton "Rex" Nettleford. That summer of 1982 was a very significant one for the NDTC. The company magnificently danced on stage, celebrating its twentieth anniversary. The great Professor "Rex" Nettleford was a very influential member of the faculty at Mona, later rising up through the ranks to vice-chancellor of the university in 1998.

Between classes at the university, I particularly enjoyed the daily exhilarating party politics discussions and cultural debates on campus. In the canteen, while munching on *bammy* (a cassava treat) and fried fish or some other island delicacy, my classmates from Brooklyn College, students at Mona, professors, and comrades from Jamaica would examine, analyze, and theoretically solve the human condition. I was particularly concerned with the plight of poor and working-class single women on the island. Who would have thought, twenty-nine years later, I would visit Jamaica on December 29, 2011 and witness Portia Simpson Miller, People's National Party (PNP) president, become the island's prime minister for the second time. Portia Simpson Miller became Jamaica's first female prime minister in March 2006 after party delegates appointed her to the position when P.J. Patterson retired. However on December 29, 2011, the people of Jamaica elected her overwhelmingly in its general election. I believe her powerful presence alone will motivate women to become actively involved in creating their own successes in Jamaica and around the world.

I have always found Jamaica's natural beauty awesomely breathtaking. It simply has some of everything exquisite: a rich history, colorfully diverse people, one captivating culture, Blue Mountains, majestic cliffs, gorgeous river falls, clandestine caves, provocative beaches, countless lakes and rivers, luscious forests and botanical gardens, exotic fruits and fishes, cassava, breadfruit and plantain, infamous ports, sensuous sunsets, ripe bananas and yummy yams, succulent cane, Red Stripe Beer, an assortment of rum products, ackee and saltfish, mineral baths, inviting tropical weather, and righteous reggae music playing in the immediate distance.

This paradise on Earth nurtured David C. Hurd to manhood. But at the age of twenty-two, he left this wonderland in search of freedom and justice. In an undated diary note, he writes, "*It is hard to stand up on both your feet and be independent there* (Jamaica)." Why did he leave? Papa said the reasons for leaving Jamaica were quite complicated, but he could answer that question simply. The increasing adversity experienced in a declining Jamaican economy pushed him to relocate to a place celebrated for its prosperity and growth opportunities.

For the longer more complex answer, Papa dramatically taught. Prior to Columbus discovering he was lost in the "Indies," the Tainos, a short, muscular people, lived peacefully in tune with nature in the land they called "Xaymaca." Hard to believe, but in less than a hundred years of their occupation, the Spanish brutally annihilated the indigenous peoples. Consequently, there is little evidence of their very presence in Jamaica. They are, however, showcased on the island's national coat of arms.

In 1655, England overthrew Spain in Jamaica. Papa would say the British had a "master plan" for the rich isle of Jamaica, which included making Mother England quite wealthy and more powerful internationally. The need for cheap labor became the most pressing plight. Initially they imported white indentured servants from Europe to work the land. Indentured servants were poor people contracted for a fixed period of time. They worked only for their passage to the Caribbean, room, and board. Papa had heard that the British also emptied their jails, sending convicted prisoners to work off their sentences.

Papa said, "believe it or not, people were sometimes kidnapped from the streets of Europe to meet England's urgent need for cheap labor." However, these methods did not supply sufficient numbers of servants for their grand money-making exploits. The British turned to the birthplace of humanity and began "using" Africans en masse. Africans were robust people, familiar with agriculture, skilled in herding and crafts, and accustomed to hot weather and hard work. Africans could not escape and disappear into the local population easily because of their high visibility: skin kissed by the sun. There also seemed to be a "limitless supply" of Africans in Africa. Unlike the white indentured servants, Africans did not have the protection of the English mother country and crown. Unlike the Tainos, Africans were not familiar with the Jamaican terrain. "

"So, using the most advanced weaponry of their time, the greedy booty seekers pitted tribe against tribe and viciously uprooted Africans from their native land. They horrifically tore apart families and villages," Papa would say. "Unknowingly, the British created a 'super-people' (a physically strong people with a higher spiritual consciousness) in Jamaica," he said. Papa described events of the Middle Passage as he saw them. "Before putting Africans on the slave ships, they were shackled together and marched in the scorching sun for what must have seemed like an endless number of miles. The weak ones died and their bodies were cast alongside the road. At the end of that journey, the captives were thrown in dark, dank, and dusty holding pens in Africa. The weak ones died in those god-awful places. The survivors were packed together on the ship's deck. For what probably felt like years, they lay compactly chained together, bathing in each other's blood, vomit, and excrement."

Papa dramatized further, "During that long and wicked voyage to the 'new world,' the enslaved suffered terribly in the belly of the beast. Ship's crew members threw the extremely sick and the dead overboard for the sharks to devour for dinner. Once in Jamaica and 'whipped into shape,' for the sugar plantations and cane fields, the weak ones died. Sold into slavery for a lifetime of misery and excruciating labor, the weak ones died. Enslavement of Africans spanned over 200 years, duly sanctioned by the British Crown."

Papa believed only the strongest of the strong could survive such cruelty of circumstance in man's inhumanity to man. It is no wonder so many influential men and women come from Jamaica. Robert Nesta Marley and Marcus Mosiah Garvey were both born in Saint Ann, Jamaica's largest parish on the north coast. Papa knew Garvey well. Both Marley and Garvey continue to inspire the lives of many on an international level. They were charismatic leaders who dedicated their lives to the struggle of oppressed and disenfranchised people of color.

"Because of the fighting spirit of the Jamaica people, we probably had more slave revolts than any other Caribbean island," Papa would say. "The Maroons of Jamaica are a perfect example of the strength of which I speak." Maroons, a rebellious and militarily skilled people, successfully fought the British and occupied mountainous regions, keeping much of their West African culture and traditions alive. As free men and women, the Maroons revered Queen Nanny and her brother Captain Cudjoe as their warrior heroes. They established their own government, towns, rules, and regulations, away from the large estates and plantations.

As a result of the plantations, Jamaica was a vital colony of the British Empire and once was the world's largest sugar producer. English sugar cane planters there grew immensely wealthy. Sugar was gold, and sugar plantations, each with its own processing facilities, proliferated. Between 1792 and 1799, some eighty-four new sugar estates were established, more than half of them in Saint Ann, Trelawny, and Saint James. At its peak, the British colony of Jamaica counted a total of 830 sugar estates.[4]

Through the years, the British continued to expand their empire in Jamaica, the Caribbean, and the world. It became so powerful, colossal, and affluent that Britain became known as "the empire on which the sun never sets." By the start of the 1900s, Britain controlled over 9.3 million square miles of territory.[5] The difference between the world of oppressed people of color struggling in exploited colonies juxtaposed with the world of rich white imperialists reaping maximum profits was economically and socially staggering. Papa told me on several occasions that full emancipation finally came to the island's enslaved in 1838, almost fifty years before he was born.

Though freed by law, African descendants were tied to the plantation and were extremely poor for the most part. In some areas, they had to pay rent, and rent was exorbitant; residences were crowded. Slave owners were monetarily compensated for their losses due to emancipation, but no such provision was made for the newly freed.[6] After slavery officially ended, poor East Indian and Chinese workers were strategically used to fill the manual labor gap and keep the cost of employment extremely low.

The House of Assembly, the colony's lawmaking body, refused to accept the idea of emancipation. Assembly members enacted harsh and retaliatory laws to maintain the status quo of British imperialism and rich plantocracy.[7] After emancipation, riots were common. To keep the peace while saving souls, the Baptist Missionary Society of London sent missionaries to Jamaica. They were duly warned to preach the gospel and not to get involved with island politics or provoke hostility among the coloreds.[8] The Baptist Missionary Church bought acres of land and founded "free villages" for the newly emancipated while it was in Jamaica.[9] The land in a free village was not free, however. For a moderate fee, the church sold plots of land, which were usually paid for in installments, over time. Missionaries intended to make these areas viable church communities.

Usually five acres comprised a plot, on which a three-room cottage was swiftly built. Below, you will see a drawing of the typical post-emancipation house sketched by my cousin Norma. The house had one bedroom on each side of a sitting room. These houses, I am told, were well built and extremely strong. They could withstand tropical rains and hurricanes. In fact, a few of them still stand in Saint Ann. One did not enter the house through the front door. There were no steps, only stonework at the base of the house. One entered from the rear. Fretwork, decorative designs or patterns, usually above windows or on the front door, sometimes had the name of the house or family carved into it. In the back of the house was the outdoor kitchen, where smoked meats hung and coffee was ground; the outdoor kitchen was paved. There was no indoor plumbing. Rainwater was captured in gutters. The chamber pot and privy were used for relieving oneself. On the land, allspice trees (*Pimienta dioica*), coffee, cocoa trees (*Theobroma cacao*), bananas, yams, and other crops were planted and harvested for personal use and for sale at market.

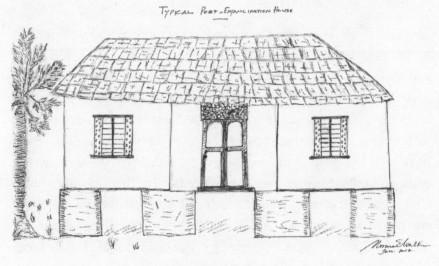

(Drawing of House)

Standfast, where David was born, was one of the free villages in Saint Ann. He grew up there with his two older sisters, Lillian and

Jemimma, and his two older brothers, Tom and Henry. Just like David in the Bible, he was the last child, the baby of the family.

David Clarence's father, David James Hurd, was born in Westmoreland. Lovingly referred to as Dear Pa, David James ministered at the Brown's Town Tabernacle Church.

(David James Hurd – Dear Pa)

Congregants said Dear Pa could preach, and when he did, he did so with such conviction and passion tears streamed down from his eyes as he verbalized God's message. David writes in an undated dairy note that his father particularly loved the first chapter of the Gospel of John, verses 1 through 14, which begins, "In the beginning was the Word, and the Word was with God, and the Word was God." Along with Pastor Dr. James Johnston and five other evangelists, Dear Pa left Brown's Town and traveled as far as Africa and Canada and back, spreading the gospel through evangelism. Ironically, Brown's Town was named after Hamilton Brown. Brown was known for his disdain of missionaries, and he even went as far as burning churches and free villages. It was Dr. Johnston, Dear Pa's mentor at Tabernacle, who was one of Brown's staunchest antagonists.[10]

Dear Ma, David's mother, Elizabeth McFarlin Hurd from Trelawny, stood only about 4 feet 11 inches tall.

(Elizabeth McFarlin Hurd – Dear Ma)

She weighed no more than eighty-five pounds and proudly smoked a tobacco pipe. Despite her small frame, she did not spare the rod when it came to disciplining her five children. She ruled her roost with an iron fist. In a diary note David said, *"the best of what I have, and what I am, I owe to my darling mother."* He cherished his family. He grew up in a solid Christian home with loving discipline, and was a member of a family who owned property. He lived in a beautiful island with perfect warm weather all year round. He ate well and enjoyed teaching and going to church at the Tabernacle as a free man. Yet David Clarence Hurd felt compelled to leave home.

Papa said that "freed" Jamaicans were British subjects who were merely surviving under colonial rule. This meant decidedly limited career choices. Once the sugar industry had drastically declined in Jamaica, the economy suffered tremendously, even with the expanding banana industry. He writes that he could strive to become a farmer or a house servant or help build the lower middle class by becoming a low-level civil servant or a poorly paid but respected teacher. David, an intellectual, reluctantly chose the teaching profession. He studied enthusiastically and successfully passed his exams. He became a pupil teacher (teacher in training) and earned a pittance in salary. He said he knew what he wanted early in life—he wanted more.

He felt the final push to emigration on Monday, January 14, 1907. An earthquake emanating fifty miles from Brown's Town literally rocked the island to its core. Within minutes, the quake demolished an entire city. The streets of Kingston in the parish of Saint Andrew stayed ablaze for days. Hundreds of people tragically lost their lives. He said when the dust had settled, a black cloud hovered over Jamaica in mourning. He was an optimist with a sunny disposition. David immediately began finalizing his exit strategy. Blessed with an adventurous spirit, big dreams, and determined to succeed and become prosperous, he began packing his bag. He believed his vision of lecturing at a prestigious American church school was soon to be realized.

America, with its forty-five states, presented a world of opportunity for him. He had heard fast-paced New York City was the most influential place for a black man to be. His eldest brother, Tom, was already there. Immigration laws were fairly lenient in those days, and arrangements could be made with the "headman" of the United Fruit Company. The boat would transport passengers along with its banana shipments to ports of call for a reasonable fee. Armed with his Bible, fifty dollars, and a letter of introduction, David Clarence Hurd set out for America in the autumn of 1907.

Papa and the New Country

"In all labor there is profit: but idle chatter leads only to poverty."

— Proverbs, chapter 14 verse 23.

Papa
David Clarence Hurd

In a letter to Avril, dated May 7, 1914, David writes:

"Conditions in America are different from those in Jamaica. There, when a man has a position if it be desirable at all, he sticks to it as long as he lives; consequently he has no outside experience. When a man comes to America, never mind what he was at home, never mind how much he had there or what he knew; when he comes here he finds that he has to begin afresh. Even the little boys on the streets seem to be wiser than he is. The more a man tries to learn here, the better he is fitted to make a comfortable living and to succeed. Therefore, people as a rule do not follow one line of work here for all time. The experienced man will try anything. He will attempt to do anything at all if there is money in it, though he never did it before: And therein lies success.

We have taken the word can't from the English language entirely and in its place we've written let's try.

There are men who insist on following one line of work even here. Those are the men who are almost always out of a job and out of cash for the simple reason that they will let very good opportunities pass by just because they flatter themselves that they have a special calling and are waiting for special opportunities along the line of that calling. While on the other hand, I know of several instances where professional men have turned their backs upon their profession to grasp opportunities along other lines. This is the land of opportunity. All a man has got to do is to lay low and grasp his as it passes by. There are half a dozen things – "Honorable" employment that I could do in New York to make a decent living and where I am employed I always make friends and strive to win the good-will of my employer. The only thing is this – Living is set on such a high scale that a man has got to spend a fortune monthly for his current up-keep. It is therefore necessary for one to observe the strictest economy in his expenditures if he desires to save and to keep some money. Here

(New York City) it is not what a man makes or earns that counts it is what he saves."

David arrived in Brooklyn, New York, in the fall of 1907, during an age of mass migration. From 1880 to 1924, more than 25 million people migrated to the United States from all over the world, mainly from Southern and Eastern Europe.[11] He came to America with great dreams of becoming a teacher. His arrival, however, corresponded with the Bankers' Panic of 1907, a time of great financial crisis. That October, the stock market had plummeted, the economy was sluggish, and interest rates were high. People pulled their money out of banks, and banks were forced to close. [12] In an undated dairy note David writes, "I had fastidiously saved up a little nest egg of "fifty dollars" for my venture to America. I placed the money deep in the side pocket of my tight-fitting trousers. I kept feeling my pocket every minute of the day to make sure it was still there because my life, my future depended on it." He writes further, "I was young and a first-class greenhorn. But even greenhorns must find a place to sleep. Like Jacob in the bible, you know, found a stone on which to rest his weary head, I declared my head was too tender for that so I went to Myrtle Avenue near Borough Hall. I was directed there. Our people all went there. There was our only refuge in the early 1900s. It was the only section in Brooklyn where colored people could maintain a foot-hold."

By 1900, Fort Greene, Brooklyn, had the only significant population of blacks in New York City. Active shipyards near that area drew free black laborers and their families. Colored School Number 1 (now Public School 67 on Saint Edwards Street) was built in 1847 for the children of black shipyard workers.[13] He lodged in several different locations while living in New York City, but his first dwelling places were in the Fort Greene section of Brooklyn. The locations I know of in Fort Greene were: 489 Carlton Avenue, 380 Cumberland Street, and 37 Lexington Avenue. After leaving Fort Greene, David

Clarence moved on to Bedford-Stuyvesant: 1915 Rochester Avenue, 1642 Bergen Street, 335A Decatur Street, and 48 Putnam Avenue (he owned the last two properties). His final stop was Crown Heights, where he owned the property at 1381 Union Street, and then he moved in with us on Lincoln Place.

In that diary note he meticulously described his first landlady (exact address in Fort Greene unknown). "*She was tall and nice looking and maintained an imperious pose. I thought at first perhaps I could let myself fall for her, she being single and having a ready-made home and all. She was a little too old for me but that I could by-pass. But as I studied her more closely, I noticed she wore glasses with a long chain attached and a wig. In those days it was not fashionable to wear a wig. If a woman wore a wig, her hair must have been a short uncontrollable mess or she was bald as an eagle. I had great pride, so I chose not to mix business with pleasure.*"

"*The landlady cleared her throat,*" He continues in the diary note, "*and started off in a calculated tone. If I decide to accept you as a roomer in these quarters, you are required to pay your weekly rent of one dollar and fifty cents in advance. There are two small beds in the room. You will occupy one. The other will be occupied by another selected roomer. There is no heating service. I supply an adequate number of quilts to keep you comfortable in bed. You will be allowed at times, to sit and warm yourself by the coal stove in the kitchen. You are not entitled to a latch key. I, your landlady, volunteer to let you in providing you make an appearance no later than 11PM.*

The toilet! Oh yes the toilet – that is in the backyard. That will entail a bit of inconvenience especially when there is snow on the ground, but you should become accustomed to this minor hardship in no time at all." In retelling the story, Papa said when he first arrived, he had no other place to go; with some misgivings, he rented the room. He shuttered and trembled with trepidation, thinking back to the conditions to which he submitted as a contracted tenant. I cannot begin to imagine how my Jamaican Papa survived with no heat through that first bitter winter in New York City.

David gives more details in his dairy note, *"I wanted a bath. There was no bathroom as such, so I appealed to that formidable person in charge. I will arrange for your bath in one hour, she said imperturbably. And in the future you must not expect to bathe more frequently than once a week. In less than an hour I was summoned. Your bath is ready, Mr. Hurd. Where? I said. There, she said, pointing at the entrance to the kitchen. She had evacuated all the other roomers who were warming themselves by the kitchen stove and heated some water for me.*

In the center of the room sat a portable vessel, large enough to accommodate the body of a person in a sitting posture. The water she poured in the tub was steaming hot. I looked around questioningly. The doors were closed and the blinds and curtains were secure. I removed my clothes and tentatively tested the water with my toe. It was inviting. Unaccustomed, I sat down uncomfortably in the contrivance. I had a squeamish feeling though. I did not trust that woman. I believe she had a secret peep hole somewhere from which she could and would surreptitiously spy on the movements of her victim roomers as they innocently in a vulnerable position squirmed around in that make-shift bathtub. I bathe quickly and got dressed even quicker."

He writes further: *"One of my many misadventures occurred almost immediately or to be exact on the night after I signed up in what began to take the appearance of a prison cell. I had an urgent call to that shed in the backyard. There was no light there. I fumbled around in the darkness. My nostrils being unaccustomed to the stench that pervaded the place, I began to sneeze. Anxiously reaching into my pocket, I grasped what I* thought was a piece of tissue. I cleared my nostrils and discarded the sticky mess. Returning to my half of the room, I discovered to my distress that the thing I had used and discarded was in reality a ten dollar bill. A ten dollar bill, my friends, in 1907 was a small fortune. (about two months rent)"

He writes in another undated diary note, "On one occasion, my cousin came to see me. A female cousin, I should say. My landlady ushered her into what she called the parlor. Then she summoned me. I could tell by her curious attitude that she was not convinced that girl was really a cousin of mine. I had no steady girlfriend at the time. There were four doors leading from and into that living room and each time I looked up there came that pussy-footing landlady traipsing out of one of those doors throwing a patronizing eye my way – as to say – I know what you are up to. You dare not sneak a girlfriend in. For a healthy young man those were dreary days. We did not stay long under the watchful eye of the sergeant major, for we had plans.

That night we headed off to see the Bert Williams show at the Majestic Theatre, 651 Fulton Street. In those days people dressed up to go to the theatre. So in our Sunday best we quickly made our way. My cousin said she would pay her own way and mine too. I refused to allow her to pay mine." All-around entertainer Egbert Austin "Bert" Williams, a Caribbean man born in Nassau, Bahamas, in 1874 and his partner George Walker were a hugely successful vaudeville act. They called themselves the Two Real Coons.[14] They were known for their minstrel shows with blackface. David, a lover of theater, wanted to experience the duo's show firsthand and pass judgment for himself.

Williams and Walker at times earned two thousand dollars a week together in the early 1900s. (in 1908 Papa's first employer in the States paid him 364 dollars a year in salary.) The partners spent the end of 1902 working on a musical production called *In Dahomey*. They strategically and successfully secured an advance of fifteen thousand dollars for this endeavor.[15] Also, along with nine other men, they founded the Frogs in 1908, an organization of theater professionals. Its mission was to form an archival collection of social, historical, and literary material for a theatrical library in Harlem on West 132nd Street. The Frogs raised money for charity, supported struggling black entertainers, and organized an annual spectacular event each August. This extravaganza, "The Frolic of the Frogs," packed the Manhattan Casino, with admission set at fifty cents. Sadly, the Frogs died along with its originators, Williams and Walker.[16]

I do not know if David enjoyed the show that night, because he did not write further about it. However, like a frog, he speedily hopped home to make curfew. As he approached his destination – *"Bang! The flood lights glared from the porch. The doors flew open and there stood the landlady her wig hat flapping in the breeze. Her eyes were wide with excitement and she was grinning as though she had just averted a tragedy. I had escorted my cousin home and was alone. I had not kissed a girl in a while and that old bat was going to make sure it never happened on her watch. I was shaken and distraught. I could have choked her!"*

He writes in a diary note, *"although bunking in a room with a strange companion who snored loudly and constantly was bad enough, my main gripe was wandering in the dead of night, in the freezing darkness frequently knee deep in snow under urgent compulsion to that miserable excuse of a restroom in the wilds of the backyard."* His next documented stop as a lodger was on Carlton Avenue. He moved from his first residence because the landlady was much too manipulative and meddlesome. He said to his dismay, he was soon to discover most landladies of that era used similar tactics.

David's housing problems were minor in comparison to his most urgent need for a job. He had been looking unsuccessfully for work for three months. He felt very poor. The fifty dollars in savings had dwindled down to a paltry fifty cents. It was time for some serious prayer. He writes, "we find ourselves on a treadmill, veritable merry-go-round, in the performance of the duties of our everyday life. To provide ourselves with our daily sustenance in this complicated whirligig of what we are pleased to call modern twentieth century civilization, our attention seems to be riveted on the murmur that persists around. What we shall eat, what we shall drink, what we shall wear, what are we going to use for money to pay the taxes, how are we going to see the insurance man, where is the cash to come from when the collector for the time payment on the furniture confronts us at the door, what we do to meet the payment of the loan on the automobile? We are bewildered. We turn to the right hand and to the left."

"We badly need a rest from all the stress and strain; forget the hurly-burly and all the fretful and carnal demands — Breathe a prayer to heaven and ask the Savior to quiet your fears and give to you that bread of life, which he alone can give. Do little deeds of good from day to day and turn to heaven and ask your Lord to build within a great, a copious fountain of that water of life, possessing which you shall not ever thirst again. So when the carnal forces of this world, in strength and power advance and bearing all the steaming, tempting viands from large and enviable stores, when they whisper in your ears and say, "come eat," be brave! Just turn to Jesus the Christ and lean on his everlasting arm."

"The Lord is my shepherd, I shall not want. In your word you promised me!" After three months of praying and looking for work, he found a job. It was not the coveted teaching position he had yearned for, but it was a job. He earned seven dollars a week, and after paying for rent, food, clothing, and incidentals, David writes his pay ensured lonely nights for a vibrant young man. He routinely went to work, came back to his room, read the *Brooklyn Eagle*, and studied his Bible.

While living in Brooklyn, he worked in several extremely different capacities. Though he carefully taught life's lessons to many, he never became a teacher in a prestigious church school. As he wrote in the May 7th letter, "*there are half a dozen things – "honorable" employment that I could do in New York to make a decent living.*" He worked on the steamer *Berkshire*, which he said was launched in February 1909. The pleasure boat, 440 feet long, sailed on the Hudson River between Albany and New York. David ran the searchlights. It was the largest passenger steamer on the Hudson. He enjoyed working on the *Berkshire* for several reasons: His brothers Tom and Henry also worked on the streamer, the pay was good, and the job kept him employed for eight months of the year.

(The Three Brothers – Henry, Tom and David)

David left the *Berkshire* and began working for Lozier Motor Company in 1914 because he was planning to marry his beloved Avril. Lozier offered less pay but better hours for a family man. He says in his letter dated May 7, 1914, "*I am employed by the "Lozier Motor Co" and I work in the sales-room and sometimes in the mechanical shop where I get chance to learn something about the mechanism of a motor-car.*" Lozier cars were ultra-expensive luxury automobiles. A Lozier 1914 Type 77 was entirely pinstriped in gold and, at one point during its production, in 24-carat gold.[17] I do not know exactly what he did for Lozier, however; his marriage certificate indicates his profession as engineer. David Clarence was classy, clever, and loved the exclusive. Though he owned several luxury cars, he never learned to drive one. He did not stay long with Lozier, because they declared bankruptcy in 1915.

During the early years after his arrival, he worked as a tailor. David, the consummate creator, could design a suit, make the pattern, and whip up the outfit in a couple of hours. He proudly made original pieces of clothing for his own children as well. According to the 1915 Census, he worked in a garage as a laborer. In the 1920s he was employed as a custodian for a billiard parlor. In the 1925 Census, David's employment is listed as "janitor." In the 1930s he worked as a doorman. During the Depression, he worked at the Brooklyn Navy Yard in Fort Greene. As a laborer, he was part of President Franklin Delano Roosevelt's Works Progress Administration (WPA). One of the New Deal agencies, the WPA provided jobs and temporary relief for the unemployed.

During the 1940s he owned and operated a rooming house on Putnam Avenue, in Bedford-Stuyvesant. The whole family pitched in with him on that endeavor. In the 1950s, he worked at Carnegie Hall as an elevator operator. Carnegie Hall, the world-renowned concert hall, has featured some of the greatest artists, from Marian Anderson to Paul Robeson, and from Duke Ellington to Billie Holiday. Papa met a few celebrities there. He regularly told the story of how a famous composer, conductor, and musician working there suddenly stopped giving him the usual gratuity. Somehow the conductor had found out that Papa was a landlord and a homeowner, and he abruptly discontinued his generous tip giving without saying a word. (In addition to the rooming house on Putman Avenue, Papa also owned a residential property blocks away on Decatur Street.)

Papa was never monetarily wealthy in America, though many believed he was by the way he carried himself. Everything he had, he worked exceptionally hard for. He believed in planning, budgeting, saving, preparing for, and investing in the future. As we look at his entire life, it can be said Papa's life was rich in experience. In the early days before meeting Avril, David appeared to be an extremely serious young man, willing to forgo short-term gratification for long-term bliss. He routinely went to work, read the paper, and studied his Bible; only occasionally did he attend a community function or recreational activity. Friends and relatives intimated that what he really needed was a wife.

He believed in taking his time and using discernment to find the love of his life. He ignored those who wanted him to rush into marriage. Call him picky and hard to please if you wish, but the fact of the matter was, he knew what he wanted in a spouse. He writes in a letter to Avril dated February 24, 1914: *Before I got interested in you I was fighting desperately with myself. You see, I am in America and there are hundreds of apparently charming girls here who would attract almost any man, especially if the man happens to be one who looks on the out ward appearance alone.*

They are possessed of beautiful features and well shaped forms, together with a keen appreciation of their own powers, and the ability to use all their fine points to the best advantage. But I do not judge of a girl now as I would years ago. . .

It was extremely important to David Clarence, at twenty-eight years old, to be equally matched with a God-fearing woman. She would cherish key values, as he did: the love of God, family, church, and community. His wife would beautifully complement him and would enjoy cultural similarities and creative activities. They would care for one another, compromise when necessary, and keep the lines of communication open, while actively listening to each other's needs. He stresses these points in the letters.

David was a romantic. He understood that when a couple put God first and experience the powers of deep true love, while continuously working on keeping the marriage alive and strong, the impossible is possible. He believed, "a truly good wife is the most precious treasure a man can find. Her husband depends on her, and she never lets him down. She is good to him every day of her life." He waited and was rewarded. A good wife, Avril personified the text in Proverbs chapter 31. She was far more precious than jewels.

He believed that he would rather wait for the right woman than rush into just any "flimsy relationship." He kept the faith on building a solid Christian foundation with a soul mate. In a diary note he writes, "When I was younger, in the community in which I was reared, the study of the scriptures was an integral part of my daily life. And not only mine but the lives also of those who lived ~~for miles and miles around~~ around and about. We worked at it in the Sunday school, in the school we attended on week days, and none the less in the privacy of our homes. The gentlefolk that dwelt around those well remembered hills and those who occupied our verdant valleys took pleasure day by day in turning diligently the pages of the sacred book.

Reading constantly story after story, and storing the essence of these stories in their hearts and minds in order to be prepared in due process of time to repeat them accurately to the young, or to defend themselves in some heated ~~argument~~ scriptural controversy, or in some friendly argument, or perchance some heart stirring religious discussion. There were few in our community who were incapable of understanding and quoting long passages from the bible. Chapter after chapter could be recited by ~~merely~~ many if called upon. And the stories of the Old Testament together with the Gospel of the New were familiar to the smallest child.

It was imperative that the woman he married, the young lady he took as his wife, be a good Christian, well versed in the Bible. She would lovingly teach their children the Word. Avril Louise and David Clarence did not consummate the marriage until their wedding day. For nearly a year, they not only wrote to each other regularly, but expressed profound thoughts, desires, ideas, emotions, and needs. They sent presents, care packages, and pictures back and forth. They developed relationships with each other's parents. They became mentally, emotionally, and spiritually intimate, while abstaining from sexual intercourse until marriage. Papa said, "if you are going to join together, bind together as one with someone, it might as well be one you respect, trust and love." Amen!

David's eldest brother assumed the responsibility of playing matchmaker for his serious single sibling. You see, Tom was involved with a young lady by the name of Matilda Cunningham (Mattie), who resided in Jamaica. Mattie had a beautiful younger cousin by the name of Avril. It took some persistent prodding by Tom before David wrote to Avril. With some nudging from his brother, David initiated a pen pal courtship, but only after seeing her picture. He was twenty-eight and she was seventeen.

Avril Louise Cato, like David Clarence Hurd, was born in April. She was born on the 11th day of April in 1896, in Port Antonio, in the parish of Portland. Port Antonio is a delightfully quaint shipping port, known for its pure loveliness and its banana industry. Compared to Papa's family, Avril's family was quite well-to-do. Her father, David Alexander Cato, had been born in Cuba. I remember hearing that he became an orphan at a young age. His adopted father, John Cato, was a cigar maker.

(David Alexander Cato – Papi Cato the Odd Fellow)

David Alexander Cato, the tobacconist, subsequently moved to Jamaica, inheriting several properties, including a cigar factory on West Street. All the tools for superb cigar making were daily utilized inside this establishment: barrels of different types of leaf tobacco, cigar tables, cutting boards, baskets for drying tobacco, molds and presses, cutters and knives. "Papi Cato," as my great-grandfather was called, also owned two cigar shops. The finished tobacco products were sold at Prospect and Cottage Shops in Port Antonio. In David's March 15th letter he tells his beloved, " *As I write, I am smoking one of your father's cigars.*" Papi Cato also owned several other properties: a two-room cottage at Red Hazel, Prospect House, Cottage House, and land at Sea Side.

Tall, handsome, and impressively built, David Alexander Cato was a member of the Fraternal Order of Odd Fellows. This group of prestigious men honored friendship, love, and truth. Very generous by nature, he religiously loaded up his horse-drawn buggy every Easter season and delivered baskets of bun and cheese (bun is made with raisins, cherries, and mixed spices - slices of bun are traditionally eaten with cheddar cheese) to the almshouse. Relatives said it was a combination of Papi Cato's overly generous spirit and bad management during his terminal illness that resulted in his businesses dying along with him in 1932.

(Rosamond Sutherland Cato – Mami Cato with Papi Cato)

Rosamond (Rosa) Theodosia Hardarang Sutherland was delicate, petite, and attractive. We believe her father and mother, Edward and Clementia Sutherland, hailed from the French West Indies; possibly from Haiti, because of its proximity to Jamaica. Rosa moved to Jamaica as a teenager. There she met David Alexander Cato. They were married on October 22, 1891, in Christ Church, Portland. She was twenty-three years old.

Mami Cato bore him eighteen children, including but not limited to Avril Louise, Rebecca Ann, David Alexander, Kathleen Tensa, Roslyn May, Valda O'Neil, and Noela Noelane. She also birthed two sets of twins and a set of triplets. (Only three daughters survived to adulthood—Avril, Rebecca, and Roslyn.) In between her own pregnancies, Mami Cato practiced midwifery, caring for neighborhood women during pregnancy and childbirth. Ironically, she died in childbirth with twins. Though I do not know exactly when, I do know Grandma Avril had already emigrated to the States when her mother died. Great-Aunt Roslyn, Avril's baby sister, was still in Jamaica. She said her mother's funeral was the most heart-wrenching sight she had ever witnessed. As she closed her eyes while telling the story, she vividly recalled the tiny white coffins where her siblings were laid to rest. Mami Cato was buried at Sea-Side, in between her two baby girls.

Avril was Mami and Papi Cato's eldest child. She spoke only English fluently, although her parents were trilingual. During private adult conversations, the Catos spoke Spanish or Creole to each other, so the children could not understand them. Though Grandma only spoke one language, her vocabulary was incredible. As a girl, she attended an excellent boarding school, founded in 1882 by a Baptist minister, Reverend William M. Webb. The first institution of its kind, Westwood High School, at the time "for girls of color," is located in Stewart Town in Trelawny. To get to school, Avril would board a boat in Brown's Town to travel to Falmouth. In Falmouth she would travel by buggy to Westwood. Her father always stressed the importance of getting a good education. He had some money and gladly paid for her schooling.

In addition to studying the scholastic basics of reading, writing, arithmetic and the social sciences, Avril learned how to be a lady. The study of etiquette entails much more than understanding table manners. Roslyn often bragged about her big sister's first-class education. Avril's studies included understanding musical theory, playing an instrument, classroom singing, needlework, and personal deportment. Students were prepared at Westwood to ultimately sit the Senior Cambridge Examinations. While in attendance, Avril wore a smart uniform and mingled with other progressive young women. It was there she befriended Amy Ashwood, Marcus Garvey's first wife. In those days, color and class determined who could attend the best secondary schools and the most prestigious private schools. Papi Cato was unwavering, remarkably so, in his decision to send his eldest girl child miles away to learn. She had already graduated from Westwood when David Hurd's first letter arrived.

(Original envelopes)

David's life was empty before writing to his Dearest Avril. Avril's letters kept him entranced and excited. He wrote very eloquently and regularly to Avril for nearly a year, beginning in October 1913, from his apartment at 380 Cumberland Street. Curious to see the home of his inspiration, I decided to take a walking tour of the old neighborhood. It was a crisp yet sunny fall Saturday in Fort Greene, Brooklyn. Yellow, orange, and red leaves were strewn on the sidewalk. Diverse groups of people bustled all around me. The scrumptious aroma of international cuisines enticed my already satiated stomach.

I started my journey from Brooklyn Technical High School, one of the three specialized science high schools in New York City. The school is located directly opposite Fort Greene Park, the oldest urban park in the United States. As a Technite back in the 1970s, I was one of the first girls enrolled there. I realized on the day of my journey that I might have unknowingly traveled down some of the same streets my Papa had walked. How amazing! I leisurely strolled down DeKalb Avenue to Cumberland Street, imagining what things were like in the early 1900s: women modestly dressed, wearing long coats and dresses and wide-brim hats; men sporting tall top hats, conservative suits with shiny pocket watches, drove horses and carts. Candy-cane striped barber poles slowly twirled and there were numerous trolley station stops along visible tracks—and of course there was the infrequent but most popular motor car. As I turned down Cumberland Street, I noticed the street sign indicating the Historic Fort Greene District. I was excited! This designation meant that the exterior of the houses were deemed historically and architecturally significant and are being carefully preserved.

However, when I arrived at a street named Atlantic Commons at Cumberland Street, to my chagrin there were no more historic designations. My Papa's former residence was no longer there. I subsequently learned that the property 380 Cumberland Street (block number 2005, lot number 69) had been demolished on June 6, 1967. In its place sat a small part of the bright, clean, well-kept recreational area with an English-sounding name—South Oxford Park—completed in 2006. That afternoon I saw energetic adults playing tennis, children enjoying themselves in the playground, teenagers playing basketball, and seniors relaxing and reading on park benches. I know one thing is sure in life, and that one thing is change. Even though I did not get to climb the stone steps at 380 Cumberland Street, I did knowingly walk in my Papa's footsteps that day.

(Nicholas Cowenhoven Maps No. 101 & 113 –
showing blocks and lots in Fort Greene.)

CHAPTER III
Papa's Letters to Grandma

"And if I have the gift of prophecy, and know all mysteries and all knowledge; and if I have all faith, so as to remove mountains, but have not love, I am nothing."

— *1 Corinthians, chapter 13 verse 2.*

Grandma
Avril Louise Cato

My Inheritance
The Letters

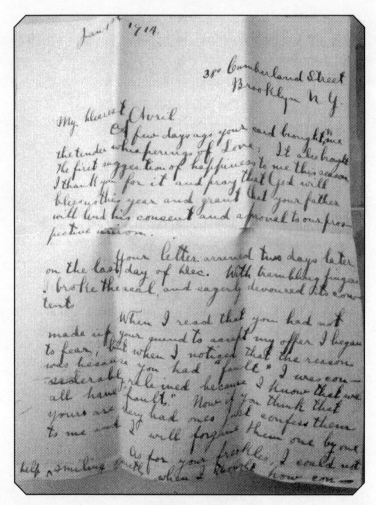

(An Original Letter)

I have digested and enjoyed Papa's letters by myself for the past ten years. I have published this book in time to celebrate the passing of 100 years since his very first letter. I felt compelled to share his warmth, wisdom, and spirituality with the world. Enjoy!

Autumn Letters

Autumn is harvest time.

After months of hard work it is time to reap benefits.

David Clarence Hurd began writing to Avril Louise Cato in October of 1913. Unfortunately I do not have any of these autumn letters. He had spent years preparing himself spiritually, emotionally, intellectually, physically, and financially. He was now ready for a helpmate. These first letters to Avril, I suppose were introductory.

Winter Letters

Winter is reflection time.

(The Christmas Card Avril sent to David in 1913 – Papa wrote these words on the back of the card, "This is the first gift I received from my ever loving and beloved Avril. I have treasured it through the years.)

David has formally introduced himself to Avril and begins to seriously consider her. Could she be the one?

In the first letter I inherited, dated January 1, 1914, he expresses the importance of meeting Avril's family and having her dad "size him up." He is confident he will pass the test, once given the opportunity. Time and space granted David and Avril many moments of reflective meditation.

SPRING LETTERS

Spring is budding time.

Before springtime, he greeted Avril in a letter with the usual "My Dearest Avril." By April 2nd, he had strengthened the ties that bind by adding, "My own Dearest Avril," and by May 17th Avril was "His only love."

(May 17, 1914) "If you were but with me my "Love" life would itself revolve into a very paradise. We could to each other imitate the birds:- softly cooing, gently wooing breathing tender words of love, each into the other's eager listening ear."

SUMMER LETTERS

Summer is the warmest and sweetest time of year.

These letters come less frequently and are filled with heightened excitement and anticipation. Their approaching wedding day is scheduled for Wednesday, August 26, 1914, in Port Antonio. The happy couple plan to meet physically for the first time the Tuesday before.

David had originally planned to marry his bride in October, celebrating the one-year anniversary of his very first letter. His boss at Lozier denied his initial request for vacation time. He allowed David to take leave in August during a relatively slow period at work. The revised plan entailed David traveling from New York by boat to Port Antonio and arriving on the 25th of August. He would meet Avril and would celebrate with the family during an evening wedding reception. In a traditional ceremony at sunrise, David and Avril would officially wed on the 26th. Quickly they would say their goodbyes to family members and friends, and then board a ship to New York City.

Jan 1ˢᵗ 1914.

380 Cumberland Street
Brooklyn, N.Y.

My Dearest Avril

A few days ago your card brought to me the tender whisperings of Love: It also brought the first suggestion of happiness to me this season. I thank you for it and pray that God will bless us this year and grant that your father will lend his consent and approval to our prospective union.

Your letter arrived two days later on the last day of Dec. With trembling fingers I broke the seal, and eagerly devoured its contents

When I read that you had not made up your mind to accept my offer I began to fear; but when I noticed that the reason was because you had "faults" I was considerably relieved because I know that we all have "faults." Now if you think that yours are very bad ones just confess them to me and I will forgive them one by one

As for your freckles, I could not help ^ smiling quietly when I thought how con- scientious you are in admitting them. I think for this reason, if for no other, I shall cherish a special little liking for those same freckles that you think are such gross faults.

I admire your modesty, and I am glad that you are so young. I always believe in a youthful marriage for a girl for then she has a chance to blossom fourth into the most charming flower of womanhood.

I observed what you said about returning the Photo. That I will do just as soon as I can get the artist to make a bust copy of it. You would not expect me to get along now with-out a likeness of you? Would you? As for your dying, I don't know what put that idea into your head. Let us think of life, for that is here and now: But death is where? We do not know but he will come to us in time unbidden.

Don't you bother your head about going out to work. If you marry me, you will be marrying a "man".

You would not like to make New York your home you say: - Well, listen, I love Jamaica and would live there tomorrow but doubt very much the chances for making a living there. Here, I am sure of my ability ^ to secure a livelihood. Of course the world turns round and conditions change occasionally. I can not tell what may happen in years, but just now my only apparent hope for a living, is here –

Now listen my Dear. "I Love you" and would like to do anything that would in your judgement and mine, help our cause. I want you for my wife and when we are married; whenever any problem crops up, I shall expect you to help me to solve them.

I am going to lay the conditions of certain circumstances that concern me before you and ask you to send and tell me what I shall do.

I was in Jamaica less than a year ago. You intimated that I might take a trip now. I think that that would be the surest way to win your father. I got a letter from Mattie and she sends to say the same thing. Only she went on to say that I could get a job on one of the boats that run out there and make a few trips. I should not like to do that. In the first place, I would not work on any of the little cheap boats that run out there: Then again it would lower my dignity and humble me in the eyes of your father.

Now my regular job opens up in March and I have to be there without fail. The only time that I could come down would be in the month of February, and then, I would just hate to buy a round trip ticket, run down, pay a flying visit, see yourself and your father and turn right back. I may not even have a long enough time for your father to see enough of me, so that he would be able to satisfy himself that I was the right sort of a chap to marry his daughter:

If the month of February passes I cannot come again until October.

Now what I want you to tell me is this. Do you think it will be advisable for me to make this flying trip in February when I will have but a week with you, or must I remain until October when I can stay for a month or two if necessary. When I should have better chance to impress your dad and to convince him that I am different from that other New York man and that I truly and honestly desire to marry honorably and take you from him in a real gentlemanly manner.

(he writes on the side of the page) compare this page with the first one and note that I am writing worse and worse as I proceed.

Is it possible for us to keep up a correspondence until October without seeing one another and at the same time keep your Dad in the dark? Is there no possible way to tell him and also give him the assurance that I have made up my mind to come out and see him personally and give him the opportunity to "size me up" It is not expedient for him to give his final consent until he sees me. I really don't think that he would refuse you to me after I talk to him because I am a man, and capable of talking like a man and acting so too.

I am willing to do anything. If you wish me to come out now, make a flying trip to see you, although it is inconvenient to me and would upset some of my plans I would do it. But if you think we could run along until October, it would be more convenient to me and in the end would prove more satisfying as I should then have a lot of things off my mind and would be better able to court and entertain you and having also a longer time to do it in.

Kindly weigh the matter in your pretty head and quickly send and tell me what you think

Did you show your mother my letter? If so what does she think? I hope she is in favor with us.

Why should the ocean stretch its vast expanse between us? That is the only thing that makes our courtship difficult. Let us however not rebel. Our destiny will work itself out. There is nothing can successfully stop the mighty rushing flow of love. Ours is a romance which like those in the popular novels will come out right in the end.

Is your father a hard man? I think not. I believe he will give you to me and finally pronounce his benediction at our wedding.

You speak about my long letter. Please send and tell me if they bore you and I will make them shorter.

Don't you speak about my being educated above your mark. The only thing that I have a larger proportion of is experience. And experience come with years.

Accept one kiss "My Love" and dream of the time when my warm and manly arms around your form most tenderly will steal when I shall hold you tight and kiss your rich sweet lips – Dream of that Kiss – Our First Betrothal Kiss.

Yours in Tenderest Love

D.

{David Clarence Hurd}
February 12. 1914

380 Cumberland Street

My Dearest Avril

You have been playing tricks on me and I ought to be terribly angry; but at the receipt of your last and conciliatory letter, I was forced to suppress all the rising evil and displeasure that seemed to have been in process of accumulation in my heart, and give way to a rather pleasant smile of gladness; so the significance of your lines became clearer and still clearer to my consciousness.

You had dealt me a blow, which I do not think was premeditated; but which hurt nevertheless.

Since I read and digested the contents of that short cold, crisp, urgent little note in which you seemed to be so carelessly stern and heartless, my mind and heart and soul – indeed my whole being seemed to have been tossing about in a restless and unsettled condition like the turbulent waves of a mighty raging tempest.

When I realized that you not only held my proposition cheaply, but actually and flatly turned it down; I suffered for a time an intense degree of mortification. But by the exercise of the strongest power of will I ultimately succeeded to rid myself of that deep feeling of chagrin which settled over me like a pall, and finally started to make an effort to think over the situation from a reasonable view point.

Of course, I firmly believed that all was over: But on the other hand I remembered that you had not received my first of Jan.

letter before you dispatched that discouraging note so I braced up, hoping against hope that after receiving that letter, it might be a sort of an influence in again changing your mind in my favour.

As time passed and I did not hear from you I was once more tasting the bitterness of woe. I wanted to write and plead with you, but my pride would not let me. I convinced myself that if I was down there I might be able to bring you around with arguments; but being so far away I was sure it would be a failure.

I wanted however to find out what could happen in so short a time to change your sentiment. My curiosity overcame me so I made that question as to the reason for your refusal of my proposal the feature of my response to your "Idle Note"

"My Sweetheart" your letter was to me like real food after a considerably severe period of starvation and today my heart is light with peaceful satisfaction.

Love is the bitterest of all the sweet – I should say "delicious" –things that I ever meddled with; but when one has tasted the bitterness of it and that experience passes, the pleasure that its sweetness brings, baffles my pen to deficit

How painful was the thought that "I had lost you" – had lost your regard – had lost all chance of winning your love – the thing that most I crave. But pain has turned into pleasure for now you've reassured me and more than ever <u>Dearly</u> you are mine – "My Little Girl" Would that the day is near when truly, warmly, sweetly and serenely I might say "My Little Wife"

"Dearest Mr Hurd" – This is the way you addressed me. You have given me the benefit of the "Dearest" but why <u>Mr Hurd</u>? That seems so stiff and formal. Please soften Dear and say when you write My Dearest D. The members of my family and also friends who know me well; They call me that. It sounds quite familiar and affectionate, but it would sound like music if it comes from you.

How are you feeling now? I am very sorry that you are ill; and more sorry that I can do nothing – can be no assistance, being so far away, but do cheer up "little one." Let us hope that you will be benefited by your trip to, and your stay in Kingston: and that having seen a good Doctor he will be able to set you right so that you will once more be cheerful having rid yourself of that "sick of self" feeling which was so much the cause of my late unhappiness, my great discomfiture.

You are enthroned in my heart. You spoke of my taking you back to my heart, I could not cast you out. I want to have, to hold, to love you forever and a day as the song says.

The time between now and October will seem like an eternity. The happiest moment of my life will be on that day when I shall see you for the first time: and, gazing into those bright dark eyes of yours, and seeing the light of fond affection beaming from their lovely depths, and feeling that thrill as it passes through my frame; and being unable to control my emotions I take you in my arms and crush you to my breast and kiss your lips. - !! That will be the happiest moment of my life – Oh pray that this will be. You crave happiness! So do I. Then let us await the time when we shall together sip happiness from the same cup.

I shall be delighted when you send that picture for me. Soon as I get it I will see the artist and have a large painting made from it just like the life – size bust I have of myself.

With a large bust painting of you in my apartment, it will be a great comfort to me. It will be life-like only that its poor dumb mouth will not be able to speak words of endearment to me.

You did make me unhappy Dear, but that is past, and when I meet you, I may be inclined to take it out of you as you suggest, but I will omit the suggested whipping. I shall be more tender yet not less effective in my exaction.

I do wish that you could persuade your father to allow you to come to New York but the chances seem to be rather slim for though it is slightly possible, I think it is hardly probable that your dad would let you travel so far. – But let us hope, and keep on hoping for the best.

I have accepted your 1000 kisses and have them all put up where they will keep good, so that I will be able to turn them over to you good and hot when we meet. I shall enjoy handing them over personally for then I will make sure that they reach the mark so that there will be satisfaction all around.

Hoping that you will be good and kind and considerate in the future – hoping that your health will be all right shortly – hoping that you will always think and sometimes think dream of me – hoping that you will write quickly and not keep me in grave surprise – hoping that it won't be long before we will be together

I remain

Yours with fondest Love

D.

David Clarence Hurd

February 24 · 1914.

Cumberland Street
Brooklyn, N.Y.

My Dearest Avril

I did not expect to hear from you already, but as I can think of nothing, talk of nothing without having my line of thought disturbed by insistent remembrance of you, I resolve to concentrate my heart, my brain for a while entirely on her who has the power to make me happy or to cast me down into the darksome depths of despair.

My head is full, my heart is overflowing, my pen is ready, paper is convenient, and ink is near by: All I have to do is write.

My evenings now-a-days are spent in pleasant quietude, and as they drag their tardy moments by, my heart aglow with mingled joys and pains would burn; for you are near to me 'My Love' so near, yet as I meditate, I realize 'how far' – yes, far – An ocean lies between – vast and turbulent stretch of ocean wide that mocks us in our love.

You are the Queen that rules in regal stateliness over all my thoughts. The first to come to me at early morn as I awake from peaceful sleep; the last that tarries in my mind as late at night, worn out by toil I quietly retire to rest.

But thoughts of you are sweet. Imagination brings you as a fond companion in my waking hour, when all the world is busy: And when the shades of night around my dwelling fall, and fast in sleep I lay; a little cupid to my heart would bring sweet thoughts of love, and grand and joyous and fantastic dreams of happiness and bliss.

My heart was hard, I never learnt to love. I could deify the charms the loveliest girl might have; But now I find its stout cords weakening, its rock-like stubbornness right now is yielding. I wonder! For you are far away, but you have cast a spell – an influence – a something that I can not here define. I always say that I am hard to get, but you have got me.

I wrote to you on the first day of January and if the old superstition verifies itself in this particular case, I will be writing to you constantly throughout the year until such time as we shall meet when writing will be – for the time being – unnecessary.

I calculate that if we are to keep the flame of our affection burning it is necessary for (us) to keep in close touch with each other, and that is only possible if we strive to correspond with one another as often as convenience will allow.

Before I got interested in you I was fighting desperately with myself. You see, I am in America and there are hundreds of apparently charming girls here who would attract almost any man, especially if the man happens to be one who looks on the out ward appearance alone.

They are possessed of beautiful features and well shaped forms, together with a keen appreciation of their own powers, and the ability to use all their fine points to the best advantage. But I do not judge of a girl now as I would years ago, by appearances, and these American beauties always puzzle me. There was always something about them that did not just satisfy me. They had this "Free and easy" attitude towards the males of their acquaintance which lowers their moral tone, according to my way of thinking.

I like to meet a girl who can chat and entertain to a certain degree of brilliancy when in company; yet I am gratified when I note in a girl of my acquaintance a certain touch of modest reserve not unmixed with quiet dignity when dealing with members of the opposite sex with whom she has just become acquainted.

With all the recognized charms of the American girl, there was always an unexplained yearning in my inner self for a true born "Jamaican girl." And though I have met many of these right here in New York, I have never seen one that would suit my taste – one that I could make up my mind to marry.

You see, our best girls do not leave home as a rule, and the few that you may characterize as "classy" that do travel, though they may have been all right at first, soon as they get away from home influence invariably compromise themselves in one way or the other and sometimes to such an extent as to become actually worse than the foreign girl.

Now that I have found you I am greatly relieved because I have found a damsel from my island home that is quite my equal. But what makes me feel more happy is in contemplation of that musical air which will pervade our home.

I have always loved music, but never learned to play any thing, though I have had the opportunity often. But My Dearest, I can sing, and already I begin to have visions of you 'as my wife' sitting at the piano, and myself standing – leaning over your shoulder, turning the leaves of your music sheet and accompanying your fine music with my best vocal efforts.

April you are younger than I am and perhaps there are many things that I have given serious thought to, that you have not even stopped to think about. Have you thought how painful must be the result of an unequal marriage - marriage between an uncongenial couple? Think how cheerless some young married people's lives must be after they have become so accustomed to one another that they get tired of telling the old story of their mutual affection

There are so many who are not capable of entertaining each other, or get no pleasure from it. They can not even keep up the old interest. They have no conversational ability, no musical training, they possess no wit and have no sense of humor; Life under these conditions become monotonous, and marriage unsatisfactory.

When we are married, if we have visitors, we can entertain them. If we have no company we will not get tired of each other. If you play on the piano for me I'll be happy. I'll sometimes sing and lend harmony to our home and good cheer to you. If we are tired of music I can recite for you or tell tales that will make you laugh. If I am a little weary, you can read me to sleep. Why! There are so many ways for intelligent people to pass the time away without boring each other. I know that I can make you happy and I am equally certain that you will satisfy me.

I hope you are enjoying your stay in Kingston. We are having a fearful winter. It has been terribly cold, and the snow has been continuously falling. But I try to be bright, with you as the sunbeam that entered to brighten my life.

Yours with fondest Love

D.

David Clarence Hurd.

Judith C. Lovell

March 4 · 1914.

Cumberland St
Brooklyn, N.Y.

My Dearest Avril

Your much prized letter of the 21ˢᵗ was delivered to me in due
course on the 27ᵗʰ of Feb. I eagerly perused its well written lines,
carefully noting all you said with full appreciation of the confident
tone of the missive.

The fact that you are not feeling well and can not at present enjoy
the blessings of life and the pleasures of your surroundings, only
serve to draw my affections out towards you more if possible, than
they have inclined before.

As I think of you there in Kingston, suffering, despondent – as
you said in your letter, an overwhelming desire to be with you,
to brighten, to cheer, to encourage, to caress you, seems to take
possession of me which feeling I succeed in getting rid of, only
by a supreme effort of will.

That the pain seems to scatter all over ^ your body, would indicate to
me that the Doctor has the correct idea of what the trouble is,
and has attacked it rightly at its strong hold; and by breaking
it up there, will be better able later, to chase it entirely out of
your system. I hope my theory will prove correct and work out
rightly: as my concern for your health and future welfare can only
be equaled by your own.

74

You must try to do what the Physician tells you Dearest, though it may be hard to comply with all his wishes. Try however to avoid any undue exertion and in that way you will more quickly regain your strength.

Don't remain longer than is really necessary before you have those pictures taken. Remember that the one I have here now is only a re-print from a picture that was taken some time ago. Anyway, you can use your own judgement, as a girl always likes to satisfy her own vanity. Now I don't personally dis approve of a little vanity in a girl. It really is one of the component parts of every nice little girl

As soon as I can get around I will go and see the photographer about having some more of those bust-prints made so that I can send those down for you that you requested.

I said as soon as I can get around because we have been having a very terrible time of it here. The weather is so bad. The snow is constantly falling, blocking the streets and tying up traffic; while thousands of people are suffering from the cold and many are dying from hunger and exposure.

I had sent down to you a small print of myself in a sitting posture. I noted on the cover that it is a very poor copy but the only one of the kind that I have now. After a while, when the weather becomes fine, I will take some good ones and let you have one.

I have many pictures of myself but I seldom take them sitting. Some how I never care about having them in that position.

I had thought of writing to your Mother but was not certain of the advisability of so doing. But if you think it is all right, I will shortly avail myself of the opportunity of getting acquainted with my future Mother-in law: even though it will be at long range I will not lose any chance to strengthen my fences.

I am simply longing and starving for one sight of you. Those are your words, they are my sentiments. Yes, it would make a difference: a great difference. Of necessity, however, it seems to me my Dear, as if we must tarry in the land of dreams, of hope, faith and romance. The bitterness of the suspense is intensified day by day; but it is bitterness which is calculated to make the sweetness which will eventually follow, so rare, so divine, as to savor of Heaven.

I am of a very optimistic disposition, and though things are very indefinite, uncertain and provokingly unsettled at the present time, concerning our desired engagement, still I console myself that your Dad, if he realizeds that we love each other, could not help but give his consent, if he is interested at all in your future happiness.

The main point at issue is for us to find out by studying our mutual correspondence, and to make certain, as near as we can get to the truth, as to whether we are temperamentally congenial. If we are satisfied your father is wise enough to know that it will be folly to oppose us.

The only thing that comes pretty near to having me up-side-down is this. I can not make any plans; I can not make any arrangements for the future. Not until I have an understanding with your father, as I should like to take suggestions from him. In short – I should like to make plans that would be satisfactory to him; plans of which he would approve, as he would certainly be looking out for your interest.

Patience is a virtue and all things come to the man who waits

Take care of your little heart and don't eat it out with fretting, it is precious to me. Trust your good fairy to take things in hand and arrange all your business for you in a manner that will be satisfactory to both of us.

With fondest Love

I wonder do you
Love me dear
As I love you today
I hope I trust I
sometimes fear

As runs the truce away

Mixed in with
Sweet and clinging Kisses
Yours Ever
D.

David Clarence

Judith C. Lovell

March 15· 1914.

380 Cumberland Street
Brooklyn, N.Y.

My Dearest Avril

I can hardly recover from the trance into which your last letter threw me. In your closing remark you said that you had written some nonsense, Well, if you think that is nonsense, you just keep on writing some more nonsense, for I like it.

How many times did I read over that letter? Goodness knows. I forgot the count. One thing is clear is this; The more I read it, the more my heart went out to you.

You see dear, I have starved myself and remained hungry for love so long a time that now, having given my heart to you, and hearing such expressions of reciprocity from you I am just wild with unspeakable intoxication which it brings

I am constantly praying that you will get rid of the pain in your knee; but I know that the pain in your heart has affected me here and neither of us will get rid of it until we meet and mutually dismiss it in the exchange of spontaneous caresses.

My life seems so empty; my apartments seem so vacant and cheerless. Oh! How my whole being yearns for you. How my soul pants for its mate, even as the horse pants for the fountain and the hart for the cooling streams. Oh! how slowly turns the wheels of time; and how cruel is fate; sometimes.

Sweetheart mine, every flutter of your heart, touches a responsive cord in mine. Every anguish that you feel is also felt by me. How

I toss from side to side of my large bed: thinking, dreaming, studying in the darkness of the night, in the stillness of the evening. Sometimes you are near and smiling, then I stretch my arms to hold you to squeeze you — to crush you forcefully to my breast when suddenly, you would fade away.

Spring-time is fast approaching. The snow has almost ceased to fall. The air is daily increasing its warmth. The snow is melting from the ground. All these indications of change in weather conditions make one feel how pleasant a thing life is. If only we can arrange its conditions to suit our various dispositions desires and tastes.

The poet said: - (Alfred Lord Tennyson in Locksley Hall) jcl

"In the springtime, young man's fancy lightly turns to thoughts of love." Well there is nothing on earth — or Heaven, for that matter — that is as great as love: Nothing that exercises so great an influence upon people as a whole; but more especially young ones, as Love.

Your letter to me my Darling; has quickened my pulse and gladdened by heart and strengthened my determination. It has encouraged me beyond measure. Why! — life is so hard to live when a person has no one who is interested — no one who is concerned — no one to ~~commune~~ commune with — no one to confide in. That is the reason I welcome with pleasure the happiness which comes to me through correspondence with you.

As I write, I am smoking one of your father's cigars. One of the boys running from Jamaica on one of the boats gave me a couple of them. On my dressing table stands your picture where I can see it. On my desk, in a little pile, are my letters from you, and in my heart is yourself – so that the very atmosphere around me savors of you.

During the winter, life with me is very monotonous. I get to work at half past 8 oclock in the morning and get home at 6 oclock in the evening. Having eaten my supper, I read the papers in order to get in touch with current events. Then I read a book or do some writing; and sometimes I go to the theatre or to the moving picture show. Sometimes I study a bit, especially when I have an engagement to give an address at a literary club or young men's league or guild. But for the most part, I stay at home.

I wish that I was gifted with the power to work miracles. Instead of waiting until we meet in order that the sight of me might cure you; I should stay right here and only just say the word and cause the pain to fly from you my Dearest.

I am awfully jealous of my my pictures and my letters. They come in for so many caresses, and here am I dying for the chance so much as to kiss your hand. "How I wish that I was that picture that you kiss until you fell asleep.

March 16th

It was yesterday that I started to write this letter. Today I am in receipt of another letter from you dated March 9th so I thought I would acknowledged and answer it herein.

I am glad to note that you are gaining weight. And also that your Dad has been over to see you; for I realize how cheering that must be to you although his stay was short.

I am certain that the constant spring air will act like a tonic on your system. Don't be alarmed the two months more that you have in Kingston will run out more quickly than you imagine. Keep on dreaming bright sweet dreams of me for youthful dreams most usually come true.

I only wish I could send you some of this nice cool weather along with some rain and hail that we are having just now; for it would do Kingston a world of good. Even a little snow wouldn't do any harm.

I embraced the opportunity last week to write to your Ma. I am sure she must have got the letter by this. I told her how much I needed you and asked for her advice and support.

I have put in an order for those bust prints of yours. It will take a little time to have them done, but I guess they will be ready in a week or two. I hope my letters do not tire you. I know one good thing; you have plenty of time in which to read them. The trouble is that they are so badly written, I believe they give you quite a lot of bother reading them.

I have bought an album for you and I want to put in most of the cards before I forward it. I think an album if it is carefully filled in is always interesting and might be shown with pride to any visiting guests. It will take a little time yet to make the necessary selection of desirable cards. I am uncertain as to whether I should fill it in or not; as perhaps in all probability you have a number of interesting cards that you would like to put in it.

However just as soon as I get it ready, I will mail it to you. Most of the mottos on the cards are sentiments that I would personally like to express.

May God bless you and take care of you and nurse you back to health and to the enjoyment of your youthful happiness; and hoping that whatever we do, or think, or hope for, may be blessed and overlooked by him – and praying that he will give us the joy of full satisfaction in each other.

I remain

Yours in faith in hope and in lasting

Love

D

April 2· 1914.

380 Cumberland St
Brooklyn, N.Y.

My own Dearest Avril

Your note of the 25th march, was received yesterday, and as usual, filled me with great happiness.

I am glad to say that the winter is gradually passing and will soon be gone. Spring-time is approaching; but this is a time when we have to be very careful, for the least little imprudence in dressing is likely to result in ones taking a cold.

I am getting along very well as far as health is concerned, but there is a vacancy in my life; and until that vacancy is filled, I will not be satisfied. I can not be happy.

I have mailed to you an album which is intended as a birthday gift. There are now in it, 220 cards, which I have been carefully selecting for you. I did not fill the book. I thought that I would leave space so that in case you should have any cards that that you prize you could insert them also cards that you will receive in the future you will have a chance to put them where both yourself and your friends can review them.

There is quite a number of those postals that I will have to explain their significance to you, when I get the chance to look them over with you, as they express ideas which are based upon conditions that exist here.

It has been a pleasant job compiling the book – It was indeed a "Labor of Love" I can only hope that it will please you.

Tom begs to be kindly remembered. As for Mattie – She has shown very much interest in us. She has dropped me many an encouraging line: and which ever way this affair turns out, I will have to be grateful to her.

I am always hoping to hear some encouraging news in regards to your father but have made up my mind to be patient.

I hope by this time you have got those pictures which I mailed for you last week, so your friends wont have to deprive you of the one you have left.

With full assurance of the consistency of my love for you I close with a prayer: - That God's blessing may rest upon us – that he might bring us together in loving union, never again to part.

Yours forever

In patience & in Love

D.

(No Date specified · 1914)

380 Cumberland St
Brooklyn, N.Y.

My Dearest Little Girl

This is Monday night and I am very tired as I was in Albany yesterday, 150 miles away, took the train from there at 2 oclock in the morning reached here at half past seven and just came home when Feddie reported from Jamaica with all those lovely mangoes from you and a splendid jar of preserves. I appreciate the offering very highly especially as you stated in your card that you had the personal handling of the preserves. I tasted it right away so as to be able to pass an opinion on it. It is very nice my dear. I shall relish it with keen enjoyment, also the mangoes.

This is not a regular letter but just an expression of appreciation of your kind remembrance of me. I am satisfied to know that you received the chocolates all right and more than pleased that you enjoyed them. I shall write again this week in answer to that very dear letter which I received from you a few days ago. In the meantime give my tenderest regards to my prospective Mother in law your mother and also my little sisters

Excuse the length or lack of length of this letter as I am almost sleeping over it. I am so tired Remember that I am saving the kisses for you and more – that I now how to give them.

Hoping to hear from you soon and to see you soon I remain

With tenderest love

Your Dearest D.

May 7 · 1914.

380 Cumberland Street
Brooklyn, N.Y.

My Dearest Avril

I must take occasion at the very outset to give expressions of my delight, appreciation and gratitude both to your dear self and to my "father-in-law-to-be," at the receipt of a very fine box of cigars; Indeed the best I have smoked in many a long day.

I experienced exquisite pleasure in smoking them; Not alone on account of their admirable quality, but also in consideration of the great sentiment which comes over me as silently sitting and deep in mediation I watch the smoke from those same smoking cigars curling upwards slowly towards the canopy of my room.

I am highly flattered that your Dad could so graciously join with you in recognizing me to the extent of presenting me with such lovely smokes.

My Dearest I certainly will soon have to come and look you over and see if I can do something for your health. I tell you the truth that personally I don't believe it to be any physical disability. You are just the least bit upset in your mind the same way as I am. I got a letter from Mattie which when I read it I had to smile. I had just finished reading yours. She says that you are getting as big as a barrel, while you said that you are reducing. I am inclined to think that you only imagine it. I really hope it is imagination as I would not like to know that my little sweet-heart is being troubled with unknown ailments.

Now my dear, as your father is inclined to view with favor the proposal of marriage which I have made to you, and as we are so far apart and as whatever preliminary arrangements to be made has got to be thought of ahead of time, I think that it is only reasonable for me to give you an idea of what I thought in my judgement would be practicable.

In the first place Mr. Cato would like to know what my profession is. Well really the work that I do for a living now I would not dignify by calling it a profession. I am employed by the "Lozier Motor Co" and I work in the sales-room and sometimes in the mechanical shop where I get chance to learn something about the mechanism of a motor-car.

Previously I used to run the search-light on the Steamer Berkshire, the pleasure- boat that runs on the river Hudson between Albany and New York. That was a very good job that lasted for 8 month in the year, closing down in the winter. I should be on there this season but owing to the fact that I am going to get married, and knowing that if I was on the boat and had a wife I could not spend one night with her during the entire eight months of the season When I got the call this season I failed to respond; as in my position with the "Lozier Motor Co" I go to work at eight oclock in the morning and get home at six in the evening and have all my Sundays off.

Conditions in America are different from those in Jamaica. There, when a man has a position if it is desirable at all, he sticks to it as long as he lives, consequently he has no outside experience When a man comes to America, never mind what he was at home, never mind how much he had there or what he knew; when he comes here he finds that he had to begin afresh. Even the little boys on the street, seem to be wiser than he is. The more a man tries to learn here, the better he is fitted to make a comfortable living and to succeed

Therefore people as a rule do not follow one line of work here for all time. The experienced man will try anything. He will attempt to do anything at all if there is money in it, though he never does it before: And there-in lies success.

We have taken the word "can't" from the English Language entirely and in its place we've written "let's try"

There are men who insist on following one line of work even here. Those are the men who are almost always out of a job and out of cash for the simple reason that they will let very good opportunities pass by just because they flatter themselves that they have a special calling and are waiting for special opportunities along the line of their calling. While on the other hand I know of several instances where professional men have turned their backs upon their profession to grasp opportunities along other lines. This is the land of opportunity. All a man has got to do is to lay low and grasp his as it passes by.

There are half a dozen things – "Honorable employment" that I could do in New York to make a decent living and where ever I am employed I always make friends and strive to win the good-will of my employer. The only thing is this – Living is set on such a high scale that a man has got to spend a fortune monthly for his current up-keep. It is therefore necessary for one to observe the strictest economy in his expenditures if he desires to save and keep some money. Here, it is not what a man makes or earns that counts it is what he saves.

At the present time I am living in a furnished room, where the land-lady supplies the furniture and takes care of the apartment;

all that I have to do is to go in and sleep. Every thing is supplied. In anticipation of our marriage I am thinking of getting a little cozy house "flat" and buy a set of furniture and have the place all fixed up in readiness for our occupancy; I have insisted on Tom's sending for Mattie and marrying her the moment she gets up here. He has made up his mind to do so and I believe that Mattie will be up here by June.

Tom, with Mattie of course will be expecting to live in the same house with me, except my plan is not carried, or perhaps there may be some serious objection. What I am saying is all suggestion of what I can and will do if it is agreeable. But I do not intend to go against your wish or the wishes of your mother and father. Much as I would like to please myself in this case I think first to please you and your parents as for as it will be consistent with my ability and resources.

I would have the house all fixed up here before I come to Jamaica and Mattie would take care of everything until I return to install you as mistress of the house. In the mean time, plans for the wedding would be made in Jamaica, so that there would need be no delay when I come down.

In my present position, owing to the fact that that I have not been on the job for any great length of time – I only took charge last November – I do not think that I can get a long leave of absence so we would have to have a very close reckoning as to dates, so as to expedite matters.

Speaking about your health and the effect that the winter will have on you here, I do not know what to say. I do not like the winter any more than any body else, but if you were here you would not have to be out in it. The only trouble is this; it would put us to extra expense to supply you with a winter outfit right at the start.

The only reason that I do not consider Jamaica seriously to settle down is because the place is so poor, it is hard to stand up on both your feet and be independent here for I can understand according to intimation in your letter that you are a little scared of travelling and you will think it very hard to leave your folks I do not blame you, but we will have to do the best we can

It is a tremendous undertaking to start house keeping in America; and I would not like to start to do anything at all in renting a place and purchasing furniture draperies crockery kitchen utensils and all the hundred and one little necessaries and big ones too except I am absolutely certain that you will come up with me and reign Queen of my "Flat" home.

I am anxious to please. If what I have suggested is not satisfactory - You will of course let your parents know all that I have said – decide with them what you would like what you would expect me to do; and if it is at all within reason or within the limits of my ability I shall strive to compromise.

You see we are courting under difficulties and we have got to make the best of the circumstances

I notice that you sent me the address of your little sister; I will go around and see her just as soon as I can make it conveniently.

My Dearest My heart is half eaten out with anxiety. I am only praying to see the end of this misery which will announce the beginning of our life

I anxiously await your Parents opinion and advise

Please convey to them My tenderest regard

I am yours tenderly

choked in the meshes of tenderest love

D.

I am saving the Kisses

D.

May 17 · 1914.

380 Cumberland Street
Brooklyn, N.Y.

My Dearest Avril

"My only Love"

Two days ago I received your letter in which you complained of my irregularity in writing and so, although I had just mailed a note to you and knowing further, that you must have got others from me in the meantime which were on the way, and may have been delayed (I hope none have been intercepted) I never-the-less hasten to respond in order to reassure you – to cheer you – to set your throbbing, tender, loving heart at rest. You know I am anxious to cherish, to encourage, to bless that little heart of yours because I know that "it is mine"

Above all things, you must not think that I am neglectful; for neglectfulness in this case would amount to cruelty. I know how badly I feel when a whole week runs out, if I did not hear from you: and a dose that is bitter to my taste I would not think of serving to any one at any rate, not to the girl that I love best

I am not sick dearest I am in the best of health and I weigh just as much as I ever weighed in my life – 167 pounds. You see I am not as big as my brother Tom, but I am not a small man by any means. I am tall and well set up as my picture shows. By the way have you ever weighed your self? If so send and tell me what is your weight as that would give me the correct idea of your "size." (laugh)

Returning to the matter of correspondence let me promise faithfully that I will use my very best endeavour to let you hear from me at least once a week. I will attend to it as much as I do to my religion. I can appreciate the state of your mind because my own is in the very same condition: and the great pity of it is that there will be abruptly no relief until I hold your hands in mine.

I am more than sorry that you have not yet received the album; but am a little satisfied as I notice that you have found trace of it. I should imagine that they would readily forward it from Kingston to you.

I would not urge you to go to Kingston just to have that picture taken for fear you should meet there, your old boys (laugh) although I should like very much to get a present – day picture of you so that I could have a painting made from it. Also a miniature for a tie-pin. "Here is another little smile" - While your reference to the boys is taken in the true spirit of a joke, I am old enough to know that a young lady of your standard and attainments must of necessity have admirers. If there were not those who would admire you, I hardly think that you would be the girl that I am looking for. But listen Dear, I should far rather that they would admire you as "my wife" as then I would not stand so great a chance of losing you.

I have made thankful mention in a previous letter about those "admirable cigars" I feel highly flattered at the receipt of them, and realize the great significance of the gift as coming from you with the good-will and approval of your father. Please again accept my deepest gratitude and to your father dear – "My Dad (in law) to be" – express for me in all good faith, my simple thanks.

Spring time is here. We have finally discarded our over-coats. Now we can walk or sit in the open air and enjoy the out-door pleasures of life. In Jamaica you can not fully appreciate the grandeur of out-door life, because the air is always good, and people are always up and around excepting when it rains. But here; after spending all the long months of winter behind closed doors, besides the burning stove or steaming radiator; bundled up in a heavy mass of wool or furs one is over joyed at the approach of spring and the anticipation of the good old summer time when he can go free and unhampered in the open as the birds that fly with unclipped wings among the trees, amid the new green foliage, building their nests happy in the act of mating.

If you were but with me my "Love" life would itself revolve into a very paradise. We could to each other imitate the birds:- softly cooing, gently wooing breathing tender words of love, each into the other's eager listening ear. Then we would forget that this world is a place where troubles are, where countless evils now abound. We would encourage the fair cupid both our fond hearts to entwine with his silken tender love – line, fast in bondage sweet divine. Then when we are closely bonded so our heart-throbs feel as one, we would those same hearts uncover so that cupids arrow sharp with its sure and certain aim, might pass freely through their tenderest sections, unreservedly uniting all our interests for all time. What then pleases you my Dearest would undoubtedly please me. So that you would gladly share my sorrows, pains and troubles and show interest in my woes.

Best regards to your circle. undying Love for you from your Sweetheart Lover

D.

The Kisses are in Storage

May 26· 1914.

380 Cumberland St
Brooklyn, N.Y.

My Dearest Avril

My only Love

I am glad tonight (12 Oclock) because, during the day, I received a letter from your father, in which, he acknowledged receipt of my letter and expressed his willingness that we should marry.

As you had already acquainted me with his feelings on the matter I was delighted to hear from him but not surprised. All we have to do now is to set a date, have every thing fixed so that I can dome down, marry you and carry you off. If your parents had known me already It would be so easy for you to come up and we could get married here. But as they don't, I think the most advisable thing for me to do is to come down so as to give them the great satisfaction to see you their eldest daughter honorably married.

Because I am happy at the receipt of a letter from your Dad please do not think that that excuses you. It is just two weeks ago today since last I heard from you. At that time I had three letters on the way to you and I mailed one last week as I make up my mind that I will not have you complain. But the same thing that you were crying for my dear, is the same thing that I am starving for.

You do not know how greedily I devour every word that you write to me. You do not realize that every pulse beat reminds me of you. I have chosen you for my wife to live with you throughout

95

my life. Naturally my heart, my soul is already linked to yours. My Dearest I hear from your parents but that satisfaction has its limitations. I am hankering after a line from you

You should see my frock coat, little girl, the one I am going to marry in. It's a peach It is not over long but it has very graceful lines with broad satin (brakes or) lapels and fitting snugly into the waist line and I carry it nicely as I am tall. Then my high hat is also becoming. I am pretty sure that on our wedding day you will Love me; and then let us pray that is will continue right on.

The point that is left to be settled as I see from here is when will be the date on which we shall get married? As I said in a former correspondence, under present existing circumstances I can not spare much time to spend in Jamaica as they will need me here on the job. Except I give this position up which would not be wise according to my way of thinking

Everything would have to be arranged so that I could come out, get married and return to New York, with you. If this can be carried out then the question is, When?

I was very much touched by the letter from your father. The missive was so Christian – like, expressing faith and confidence in God. It is just the kind of letter my own father would write under the same conditions

I shall write to him just as soon as I get myself together but I might just as well say here that I am highly gratified and will try to prove my self worthy in every way of you his worthy daughter

Mention me affectionately to the rest and Dearest please don't starve me. <u>Do write often please</u>

Your Most sincere and

Loving Lover

<u>D.</u>

June 10· 1914.
Please excuse blotches

380 Cumberland St
Brooklyn, N.Y.

My Dearest Avril

would

How I ^ rejoice if conditions were, so that instead of your cousin
Mattie who is at this time on the ocean coming up to Tom, it
was your dear little self coming up to me. - But fortune does not
always smile on us and when our hearts are all set on good things
we are likely to suffer in anxiety at the anticipation of them.

In imagination I can see the prize for which I long, the prize
which steadfastly I seek the prize which – "she herself-" fain
in my arms would fly (blotch) far, far away; My heart hopes,
then fails within me – This ocean wide, this time indefinite, the
great uncertainty of it all almost completely unnerves me; I
brace myself, I take courage but still my – "Love" is far away;
Yet I must through it all most resolutely turn my back and
stop my ears to all seductive and surrounding charms. I have
a "halo" bright, created round the very thoughts of my loved
one. You are my Queen and though the fog of restlessness
and fear and dissatisfaction and even doubt around the citadel
of my heart should settle dense, even then would I around my
Queen in beauteous and imaginative bliss, build castles grand,
and paint bright pictures of the scene prospective Dear; of that
moment when, with palpitating heart and forms that weakly shake
from force of natures fierce emotion; we in each other arms shall
fall insisting if for one moment thus to shut the world, its rude

intrusion out and sip from each others lips the true essence of tender, pure and lasting Love.

That will be for us the beginning of it all; and Dear, let us make a resolution even from now, that both of us each in our way will add the oil of grace that burns in the lamp of love, constantly to the original supply in order that it shall always continue to burn brightly illuminating our young lives: and when we grow old together, then it will make pleasant our way for us.

I wrote to your Dad, last evening, I suppose it will reach there simultaneously with this letter; I spoke of many little things. Among them, I made mention of your preparation for marriage, in respect to your trousseau. I know that every young person who is anticipating marriage gives a lot of time and thought to the getting together of a suitable supply of clothes. I do not know if you are out-side of the rule. Now if you were going to live with me in Jamaica, I should not have one word of advise or suggestion to give along (blotch) that line: But considering that you will be coming here, where there is such a lot of variableness and complexity in styles, I have suggested that you purchase not many dresses now but rather wait until you come up here, then you will be sure of what you do – except of course you are absolutely positive that you can have your dresses made in the same styles that prevail here. You must not be vexed at my little presumption in attempting to advise you in the matter of dress. I am sure I am just as much concerned in the way you dress as you are yourself. And I have a right to be since you are my own.

It will be a great surprise to the few acquaintances that I have in Port Antonio, when I come down to get you. They will have a pretty big guess as to when and where we courted.

There is one thing I did not think of which must be found out. It is this: - Can arrangements be made for my marriage with you without my being there? If not, it will not be practicable for me to reach there on Sunday and get married on Wednesday. We will of course have to make certain on that point. Tell your parents that I send them the affection of a son, and to your sisters give brotherly –

(Turn over)

greetings.

For your self my sweet-heart accept all that is best in me, while we long for the time when we will be as one – together – never to part

Yours ever

In the tender bonds of Love <u>D</u>

June 30· 1914.

380 Cumberland St
Brooklyn, N.Y.

My only Love

me

You must excuse ^ for having skipped a week in my correspondence.
It is however your fault and not mine. Last week I waited to
hear from you before writing. No letter came, and before I
thought how fast the week was running, the mail day passed. This
week, I started to wait but as the mail leaves tomorrow, and as
I did not get a letter today I embrace the opportunity any way,
to write tonight (10.30 o clock)

Time is passing so quickly and our wedding day is drawing so
very near, that we can not afford to permit these long lapses in
our correspondence with each other.

My Dearest I am earnestly endeavoring to have every thing
arranged on this side so that you will not have any inconvenience
when you come up.

You will notice by my last letter to your father that circumstances
has made it necessary for me to cut off six weeks from the time
of my previous reckoning, so that now there are only about seven
weeks between us

As I explained to your dad, I had a talk with my Boss
explaining my position to him, and at the same time letting him
know that I would have to have a vacation in order that I could
go home and get married. He told me that I could have the time

that I desire; but in August, when business wont be as rushing as it will be in October.

I believe you will have no difficulty in getting ready by that time, and my love besides bringing us together earlier than we anticipated it will be better for you because you will then come up here while it is yet warm, while the trees are yet green before the cold fierce winds of winter begin to blow its gusts upon us.

My head is now full of business. I have been trying to secure my furniture, and will have them delivered, just as soon as I get a "flat." I want to have the place by the first of August so that I will have a couple of weeks to straighten things out before I start for Jamaica.

I am getting a nice large brass bed for us. I have hopes that you will like it. Then I am getting or at least I hope to get for you a bureau of mahogany and for myself a chiffonier for the room. I cannot tell you all in this letter and if I did, when you get here nothing would surprise you. I am going to try my very best to make you comfortable and I hope to succeed.

Please send and tell me all the arrangements that will be made for the wedding so that I will know just where I stand and how things are going.

I have lately written three letters to your dad, explaining every thing. I hope he will coincide with what I say and what I wish

I am starving for a line from you. My poor heart is perishing within me. I feel neglected. I am just counting the days. I even lose my appetite. Now that the time is coming it seems harder to bear the suspense.

Kiss my sisters for me. Give my love to your Ma; and to your Dad, My best respects to you My Love, My heart belongs Take it! Tis thine

Tis thine all that I can give

Do I get yours? Tis all that I require

Your true Lover

& Prospective Husband

D.

David Clarence Hurd

(No Date specified —sometime in July. 1914)

380 Cumberland St
Brooklyn, N.Y.

My Dearest Avril

My only Love

I am now counting the weeks, the days, the hours. We have reached a point, where we can cease counting the months as we only have one month and some weeks. It is now past twelve oclock midnight and I have just returned from New York where I have been to see Mattie.

While I was over there, I bought your wristlet and ordered the wedding ring, both of which will be engraved with our initials and the date of our marriage, Aug.26.1914.

I must confess to you that I am tired, almost worn out. It has been a hard struggle for me, having to attend to every detail of preparation my self and having so little time in which to attend to business.

I am earnestly anxiously waiting waiting to hear what you, mother & dad have to say about the change of date. "You should Worry" That only brings us together the sooner. I do not care how small the wedding is.

I am making all arrangements for you to spend a warm winter. I have rented apartments on a very "swell" block on Grand Ave. with 6 rooms & bath; and intend to move in on the first of Aug. There are two floors in the apartments & the rooms are large airy and every thing is convenient. There is a large coal stove in the Kitchen and two "Baltimore" heaters in other rooms which will insure you against the rigors of winter. All I need now is after I take charge to order about 6 tons of coal stored away in a bin in the cellar.

I am working day and night to prepare for you sweet heart and if I can but please you I will be perfectly satisfied.

I should write Mammie but I am too tired now to write a good letter. Kiss her for me and say that I am expecting my shirt. The only thing about that shirt, she should open it all the way down in the front so I wouldn't have to put it on over my head. Regards to every one, Love to my sisters and best wishes to Dad. I am yours forever in faith in hope in devotion & love D

(No Date specified –sometime in July/August 1914)

380 Cumberland St
Brooklyn, N.Y.

My own Dearest Sweetheart

Very few more letters shall I write to you. All that is in my mind at this time is thoughts of our Meeting

If you will remember, in my very first letter to you I said that I should be ready to come out for you in about one year's time. If you will hark back to that date, you will find that the year will not be closed out since the time of that first letter to the date that is now set for our Wedding.

These have been months of hopes and fears, joys and sorrows, anxieties, anguish, and anticipations of ultimate bliss.

I should not like to have to live this over again. It is a struggle that a man needs courage as well as a girl to go through once. The idea of a boy and a girl engaged to be married and each one going through the ordeal of preparation without ever having seen each other, it sounds like a chapter from a popular novel or like a story that had its origin in fairyland.

My Dearest I must say that you are a brave girl and a girl after my own heart to make up your mind to take such a desperate chance as this. Putting your faith your hope, your trust in a man whose voice you have never heard, who has never had the chance to touch your hand, whose warm breath on your cheek you have never felt. The pressure of whose eager lips upon your own has never quickened your pulse beats or caused the blood to rush wildly through your veins. Whose arms has never clasped you to his breast and caused a touch of nature to thrill your whole frame yet you have made up your mind to love honour and to trust me in spite of all.

Let us ask God to work out in his own best way, plans for our happiness, success and future contentment.

I am more than sorry to hear that you have not been well, but I must say that it is a wonder you did not break down entirely under the strain. It will soon be over now for soon God willing you will have the right to lay your head upon my manly breast and tell me all your little cares. Then I will gently pat your heavy curls and you will be consoled. About your coat, I thought I had mentioned concerning it in a previous letter. I would not think of coming to Jamaica without it, though you will hardly need a coat at the time that we shall reach New York on "our honey moon trip." However we never can tell what new tricks the weather will have in store for us therefore it will be safer to have it. I only hope I do not make any mistake about the size. Better no coat than a bad fit. It is rather hot in the City now and I always lose weight in hot weather so if I look tall and skinny when I get there, don't be surprised, I will fatten up in the cold months of winter.

You have not yet sent to tell me what arrangements are being made for the wedding but I suppose you are still a little upset on account of the death of your sister etc. I would advise you though not to yield to nervousness but store up some reserve courage which you will need when the cry is sounded – "There comes the bride" when you will meet me before the altar where you will be the observed of all observers.

It is a funny thing that people never pay much attention to the bridegroom. All they have eyes for is for the <u>bride</u>. – It is also a peculiar fact that the groom never sees any body at the wedding except his bride.

I am supposed to move from 380 Cumberland St by the first of August, that will give me a short time to fix our place up, then I will leave Mattie in charge when I take my trip to secure you.

Don't be alarmed about coming with me to America. I shall exert myself to the utmost to make you feel comfortable and content and though you may be a little home sick at first at having to leave Mammie you will soon get to like New York and the wonders that New York holds.

I am expecting a letter this week. This is Thursday and it has not yet come but I am patient. Love to all. Mammie Dad and the rest. Very little now stands between you and an avalanche of kisses, some mighty tight hugs, and some barely audible mutterings of affection and love; all signifying that "Thy Lover hath found thee and is claiming his own.

To my Love

From her true Lover D.

(No Date specified —sometime in August 1914)

37 Lexington Ave
Brooklyn N.Y.

My Dearest "Little Girl"

I do not know what you are thinking of me at this time. A whole week has passed since last I wrote to you; And I tell you, it has been the most strenuous week of my entire life. I am fully established in our new home now and Mattie is preparing my meals and catering to my appetite daily but up to the present time she has not introduced into the bill of fare any thing like stewed mutton and garden egg. I have fixed up the house as much as I expect to do before I leave here. I shall leave the finishing touches to you. I expect you are capable to attend to that.

My Dearest, have you heard about the great European War? I thought at first that I would not be able to come to Jamaica on account of the sea fights that are now going on but I will surely come to you if I have to swim across the Atlantic

I do not wish to have any great lot of cake sent down to Saint Ann. Just a bit for my mother and sisters will be sufficient. Tell Mammie that I heard from Dear Pa yesterday. He seems to be quite satisfied with my choice and promises to meet me at P.A. (Port Antonio) You will therefore see him before you meet me.

You will come up to New York just at a time when the weather conditions will be fine and when the theatres will be reopened for the Fall and Winter Season.

Cheer up little girl. Don't think too seriously yet of marriage life. It has its shadows but it has also lots of sunshine and joy

My father thinks that you are a very brave girl to make up your mind to leave your parents to come with me to a strange and foreign country but my love you will not regret it. If you will only stand by me and encourage me in all my plans and in all my efforts, we will by all means succeed.

I have bought a nice fall coat for you I only hope you will like it. Give my love to Mammie and tell her that her son will be with her in a very short time (If the German War ships don't stop me on the sea) To my sisters, affection. To my Dad, best wishes and kind regards

To your self — My most enduring love and tender blissful kisses

While I claim the right to be your Husband Dear and True D.

CHAPTER IV
Papa and Grandma: Life after the Letters

"Kiss me and kiss me again, for your love is sweeter than wine. How fragrant your cologne; your name is like its spreading fragrance… You are as exciting, my darling as a mare among Pharaoh's stallions. How lovely are your cheeks; your earrings set them afire! How lovely is your neck, enhanced by a string of jewels."

— Song of Solomon, chapter 1 verses 2 and 3/ 9 and 10

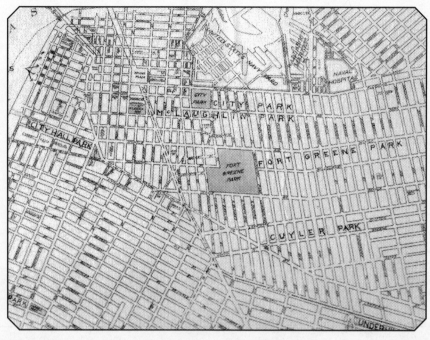

(Segment of the Map of the Borough of Brooklyn City of New York 1909)

(My story is based on bits and pieces of information and serious storytelling from family members and friends.)

Tuesday, August 25th, finally arrived. It was the date set for David Clarence Hurd and April Louise Cato's first meeting and their evening wedding reception. Organizing "the most memorable nuptial celebration and marriage ceremony" depended on many helping hands at work and took countless grueling hours of painstaking preparation. Avril's home in Port Antonio, located on the east coast of the island, is an incredible place to celebrate the love between two people. That tropical town is romantic, charming, and downright breathtaking. The Cato homestead bustled with enthusiasm and ceremonial activity. Family members, friends, and recruits anxiously readied the entire place for the groom's arrival.

Papi Cato admired the superb detailing on the dress shirt his wife had made for their son-in-law-to-be. Mami Cato carefully put the finishing touches on Avril's wedding dress by stitching its outer skirt hem. Beautiful bougainvillea and hibiscus arrangements decorated the property. Every inch of the house glistened with cleanliness and beamed with order. Outside, a gigantic white pig slowly roasted: his hair had been shaven, his carcass prepped, and his skin stuffed with a delicious blend of herbs and spices. The traditional wedding cake, a three-tiered rich black cake made with wine and rum-marinated fruits, sat on a small table. A white linen cloth delicately covered the table. Green ferns, creatively scattered around the cake, added color to its pure white iced base. The elaborately decorated cake, with handmade pink and red cascading roses, appeared regal.

The scrumptious smell of island delicacies dramatically filled the air. Gifts of rice and peas, roasted yam and breadfruit, boiled green bananas, fried plantains, curry goat, curry chicken, mannish water (a popular Jamaican soup made with goat meat, garlic, and scallions), duckunoo (cornmeal and other mouth-watering ingredients wrapped in banana leaves) totos and sugar cakes (coconut treats), sorrel, mauby and ginger beer (delicious Caribbean beverages) were brought to the house as love offerings by neighbors and well wishers.

Avril, dizzy with anticipation and sheer nervousness, checked and rechecked, packed and unpacked her grips (suitcases) several times, making sure she had included everything needed for her voyage to and life in America. I bet she asked herself whether David Hurd was the man of her dreams, or was this whole thing merely a dream? Avril's stepsister Ernestine anxiously followed her around the bedroom. She lovingly fussed and tidied up, making the bride-to-be even more jumpy than she was already. Avril said that she was so tense she wanted to run away and hide in the garden forever. Roslyn, eight years old, begged and pleaded with her older sister to stay in Jamaica and not leave with "that man." Teenage sister Rebecca moved quietly from room to room with an expressionless face and properly folded arms, watching everything and everyone. She could not wait to confront the bridegroom, to look him over and personally pass judgment.

David Hurd had been traveling almost a week to collect his beloved. Tiredness had seeped into every pore of his body. Immediately, though, a surge of power energized his entire being the moment he stepped foot on Cato property. He affected an air of strength and confidence. He appeared clean-cut, well dressed, and he was smoking one of his future father-in-law's famous cigars. Just as the bridegroom checked his pocket watch, Papi Cato emerged from behind a door. He sternly ushered David Hurd into the sitting room for "the talk." I do not know what was said during that meeting, but apparently, Papi Cato approved of him. Upon his request, Mami Cato brought Avril into the room to meet her future husband.

David's heart pounded so loudly he was convinced everyone in the room could hear its frenzied thumps. The pictures he had received of Avril were indeed beautiful, but they hid her true radiance. His queen was a fine-looking woman, and she was soon to be all his. His magnetic personality helped ease Avril's mounting anxiety. She appeared before him ladylike, reticent, and youthfully innocent. "Strength and honor are her clothing; and she shall rejoice in time to come. She opens her mouth with wisdom; and in her tongue is the law of kindness." (Proverbs 31:25–26)

Papi and Mami Cato took time before the scheduled reception to counsel the couple in "the ways of marriage." Marriage is not just about a couple; it is a blending of two families. Always move together in peace and love, never go to the marital bed angry, and serve the Lord unreservedly. After all the formalities had been appropriately handled, Papi Cato announced with gusto to all of his guests, "Vamos a celebrar!" (Spanish for "Let's party!")

(Wedding Photo – August 26, 1914 in Port Antonio – Behind
Papa is David Cato and behind Grandma is David Hurd)

Papa often told the story of how he got married the following day at sunrise. Avril rode in her father's horse-drawn carriage to the church. People lined the streets, wanting and waiting to see the extraordinary couple and their entire wedding party. That morning, my grandparents performed an amazing act of faith. They followed God's lead, believed in each other, and committed fully to the sacred bond of marriage. Methodist Minister David Parnther united the couple in holy love during a conventional ceremony. Papa said there were four Davids in attendance on the 26th: the minister, David Parnther; Papa's father, David J. Hurd; his father-in-law, David A. Cato; and Papa himself, David Clarence Hurd. A church full of spiritual men, four of whom were named David, must have been a significant omen!

After the wedding, the lovebirds readied themselves for their trip to America. Sadly, Papa did not have much of an opportunity for fellowship with his new family. He said his goodbyes quickly. He had to get back to work at Lozier Motor Company. As head of household with a new wife, his personal responsibilities became his primary focus. Dear Pa (Papa's father) laid holy hands on the couple. He prayed over them, begging God for traveling mercies. As he interceded on their behalf, tears trickled down his cheeks onto his white beard. He was extremely contented to know his son had finally settled down with a good woman. However, saying goodbye again to his youngest son was heartbreaking.

I laugh every time I think of Aunt Roslyn telling the story of Papa, Grandma, and the ship ride to New York. David had patiently waited nearly a year for his beloved. During the five-day trip on board the *S.S. Obidense,* Grandma could not keep Papa away. She played coy and would hide. Persistent Papa would find her. He was like a hungry lion that had not eaten in months. He wanted to devour his new wife whole. He had lovingly stored up thousands of kisses and hugs too. And he was determined to give them all to his "little girl" on their floating honeymoon. The marriage was consummated again and again and again and again.

By October, the original month set for her nuptials, Grandma was pregnant with their first child. She was only eighteen. Practically overnight she had become a newlywed, living in a strange home, learning new roles, and abiding by unfamiliar rules in a foreign land. Mrs. Avril Louise Cato Hurd had willingly embarked on the most challenging yet most rewarding adventure of her life. Her husband made sure the adventure never ended.

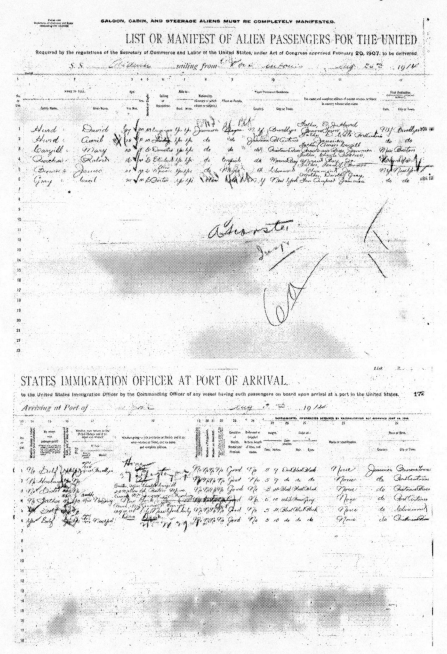

(Ship Manifest dated August 26, 1914)

CHAPTER V
This is Not the End

"Therefore, if anyone is in Christ, he is a new creation. The old has passed away; behold, the new has come."

— 2 Corinthians chapter 5 verse 17

(Papa and Grandma)

My grandparents were born in different parts of the island of Jamaica: Brownstown, Saint Ann, and Port Antonio, Portland. They did not meet and court while they both were living in Jamaica. Papa had immigrated to Brooklyn, New York, and Grandma was still living in Jamaica. They exquisitely used the art of letter writing to develop a deep, loving bond. They remained faithful pen pals for nearly a year; then they met for the first time on the afternoon before their actual wedding day.

(Papa and Grandma - 48 years after that very first letter)

Papa and Grandma lived together as husband and wife for forty-eight years until her untimely death in the fall of 1962. She was only sixty-six years old. Nevertheless they raised six children, twelve grandchildren, and piqued the curiosity of many who wondered what was the secret that kept this extraordinary Caribbean-American couple forever sweethearts. Uncle Jimmy (David James Hurd, my grandparents' first son) has a theory. They kept God at the center of their lives. He remembers seeing his parents religiously together on their knees in prayer. "O Lord, thou art my God; I will exalt thee,

I will praise thy name; for thou hast done wonderful things; thy counsels of old are faithfulness and truth." (Isaiah 25:1)

My grandparents prayed routinely. They grew together religiously. Prayer, however, does not guarantee a life free from spiritual tests and temptations. Papa and Grandma were not perfect. They had human frailties like the rest of us. My mother (Judith Marilyn Hurd Lovell, their fifth child) remembers a particular disagreement. She was in the house with brother Rodney. They were about eleven and twelve years old, respectively. Grandma was in the kitchen with Papa. In anger she forcefully threw down a glass cup onto the cement flooring by the sink. It shattered into several tiny pieces. Papa responded by telling Grandma, "you are not the only one who can break things in this house." He pelted a saucer on top of the tiny pile of glass. It smashed into bits. The two children watched in amazement as their parents broke almost every piece of glassware and china they owned. Tired from clashing and crashing, they proceeded to separate corners of the house to cool down. Following a break from each other, they calmly joined forces to clean up their mess.

After Grandma's transition, Papa declared there would never be another Mrs. Hurd. He was the first to admit he had received several romantic offers, and even quicker to inform the family that he had turned them all down. True to his word, Papa remained single for nine long years. He joined his beloved Avril in the Fall of 1971. He was eighty-six years old. Coincidentally, both Papa and Grandma were born into eternal life during the month of October- the original month set for their wedding. Grandma transitioned on October 16, 1962 and Papa on October 7, 1971.

During the early 1900s, when David Hurd met Avril Cato, letter writing (snail mail) was the only means of communication available to them. Telephone lines were not connected yet in Jamaica. Today the world is a global village. The Information Age with its technologies has brought the seven continents together with the click of a mouse and the tweet of Twitter. Not only can we talk to someone in another country from the convenience of our homes, we are equipped with mobile phones in our pockets. We can immediately communicate with the world using e-mail, Facebook, text messaging, Instagram and Skype. New and innovative technologies are readily produced and made available daily. In the midst of such exciting evolution, has letter writing, the magnificent tool that brought my Papa and Grandma together, become a lost art? Has it lost its pragmatic usefulness as an economic, interpersonal means of communication? I turned to my son and eldest child, Kwame C. Prescod, for answers.

Kwame is a technologically savvy member of Generation Y. He grew up with computers and gadgets. He loves them. In junior high school, he took apart a computer. To the amazement of his teacher, Kwame put it back together again perfectly. The computer and especially the Internet have changed our lives. Young innovators like Kwame are mutitaskers, proficient game players with numerous tag names, screen names, passwords, cell phone numbers, and e-mail addresses. The language online is unique and informal and very different from Standard English. Friendships and associations can be made simply by accepting someone as "friend" online.

Kwame believes letter writing, though not as prevalent in our lives today, must not become a lost art. "Letter writing is a permanent record," he says, "that takes time and care to prepare." He adds, "Love letters can be read, corrected, rewritten, reread, scented, and sealed with a kiss. Unlike new technology, letters are not usually extremely short (140 characters or less), written in a rush with misspelled words, impersonal, and filled with abbreviated text and emoticons, OMG (Oh My God), SMH (Shaking My Head) while LOL (Laughing Out Loud). ☺" Another point, Kwame continues, "even though we are living in the Information Age, not everyone has access to the latest technology; hard to believe, but not everyone owns a computer."

Kwame, who has a striking physical resemblance to his great-great grandfather, David Cato, has much in common intellectually with his great-grandfather, David Hurd. He too believes, *"the more a man learns in America the better fitted he is to make a comfortable living"*. In his short lifetime, Kwame has had a variety of decidedly different work assignments and is the consummate entrepreneur. Interestingly, Kwame met his wife, a Jamaican from Kingston, online in 2001. They chatted electronically for nine months before meeting face to face. He developed their romance using the art of letter writing only after going away to school in 2002. On Saturday, June 24, 2006, Kwame wed his pen pal. In the words of Yogi Berra, "it's like déjà vu all over again." Kwame and his wife still write to each other. They keep their love letters safely tucked away in shoeboxes under their bed. Maybe one day Kwame's grandchild will curiously go through his collection of letters and will appreciate the history, creativity, eloquence, and style of each carefully constructed letter. That is exactly what I did with Papa's letters. Through his letters and diary notes, I have bonded with my ancestors. I have also created an approach that will positively inspire and inform future generations.

Papa's letters to Grandma—what a magnificent inheritance! Over hot cups of ginger tea and slices of bun and cheese, I appreciate my present. In an inconspicuous corner, I often vicariously enjoy the adventures of my Papa and Grandma. As I run my fingers through each letter, yellow with time, I realize how powerful each sheet is. Papa's letters are almost one hundred years old, yet they are as strong as he was, showing few signs of age, few signs of wear and tear. I admire his penmanship. His handwriting animated the words. Each word is painstakingly perfect, each cursive stroke beautiful and rich in texture. As I read his words, literate and expressive, I can hear his voice jokingly chastising Grandma for the brevity of her letters.

I love going back in time with my ancestors to twentieth-century America. Papa's letters and diary notes are detailed and informational. I actually feel the loneliness of a Jamaican immigrant, miles away from home. I imagine the pain of a black man striving desperately to be successful in America, a foreign and often hostile place. I understand the excitement and anxiety of a fiancé planning for the first meeting of his beloved bride-to-be. I respect Papa's keen insight and knowledge. I welcome his words of wisdom, applicable to this very day and time. I honor his spirituality. He was God-centered and firmly rooted in the Gospel. As a poet, myself, I love his use of words—so impressive and expressive.

David Barton, professor of language and literacy at the University of Lancaster in Northern England, and coeditor Nigel Hall, in their book, *Letter Writing as a Social Practice,* say, "The letter as an object of literacy practice is peculiarly versatile and diverse as a carrier for text; the letter can be used to mediate a vast range of human interactions; through letters one can narrate experiences, dispute points, describe situations, offer explanations, give instructions, and so on." The book emphasizes the importance of studying letters, and letter writing of everyday folk.[18] Since the practice of letter writing is so broad and diverse, one can begin to understand a host of social, cultural, and historical phenomena.

What do Papa's letters tell us?

As a youngster, I listened quietly as the elders told stories. Papa's letters connected some of the dots and filled in some historical gaps. Through his letters, we are able to fit the pieces of our genealogical puzzle together. As a matter of fact, many members of the family had little information about our heritage and about their most fascinating past before reading the letters. Papa's letters help to keep our story alive and acknowledged.

His letters provide details on what was happening in America during the early twentieth century. We learn about the economy, social customs, etiquette, fashion, theatre, and music. We realize that in 1907 the rural South was not the only area to have outhouses;

Brooklyn, New York, had them, as well. Papa showed us that black women owned homes and effectively and efficiently managed rooming houses. When he first emigrated to Brooklyn, he rented rooms. He watched his landladies and asked them questions. In later years, Papa became a landlord himself. In his writings, he illustrates the road to a stable financial future. He advises one to be frugal, to invest, and to save.

His letters maintained the omnipotence of God and the importance of our spirituality in a material world; there are no letters where God is not mentioned or the Bible is not quoted. On the sixth page of his letter dated March 15, 1914, he implored, "*may God bless you and take care of you and nurse you back to health and to the enjoyment of your youthful happiness; and hoping that whatever we do, or think or hope for, may he (God) be blessed – overlooked by him (God) and praying that he (God) will give us the joy of satisfaction in each other.*" We clearly see from his writings that God is at the center of his life.

(Papa and his six children – seated from left to right,
Rosemonde, Ruth Andrea, Judith and Avril –
in the back row David, Papa and Rodney)

His letters honored family. David did not write exclusively to Avril. He wrote to her mother and father, as well. He believed in the importance of building a loving relationship with the entire family. He often ended a letter sending brotherly love to Avril's sisters. Family was crucial to Papa's well-being. On his deathbed, he made the family promise to always pull together in support of one another.

His letters and diary notes made mention of a man's responsibility to his wife as provider, protector, and prayer partner. Though tired, overworked, and underpaid, he could not rest until he was satisfied his beloved would be taken care of during her first winter in America. He recommends that his wife-to-be not buy clothing to come to Brooklyn; *"fashion is so different here"*. He writes they will go shopping once she arrives in America. This will ensure her comfort and warmth. It was extremely important to him to be equally yoked with his partner. Through his letters, David got to know and understand Avril. He discovered they could share a spiritual connection with God through prayer, music, conversation, and daily activities.

During the 1920s, while Papa and Grandma were living at 1642 Bergen Street, they discovered the perfect church home only a couple of blocks away. It was extremely important to the both of them to keep the Sabbath holy. At the time, Saint Philip's Episcopal Church (now at 334 MacDonough Street) was located at 1610 Dean Street. Many of the congregants were from the Caribbean, and the mission had recently obtained parish status. Papa subsequently joined the vestry of this growing parish. Vestry members create and manage the budget. They oversee church property and plan for the present and future interests and endeavors of the church. Papa was also a lay reader there. He dramatized the scripture each Sunday and sometimes conducted the entire morning service during the Lenten season. Grandma became president of the church's Saint Monica Society; a group of dedicated women who prayed for and visited the sick and shut in. Papa mentioned in his diary notes that in the community where he grew up, the study of scriptures was a very important part of his daily life. In Saint Philip's he found the ideal environment for his entire family to flourish spiritually.

His letters intimated volumes about the educational system in the late 1800s and early 1900s for Jamaicans. Not only was Papa's father a knowledgeable and literate Baptist minister, Papa himself completed secondary school. He excelled in writing, reading, and public speaking and taught for a while on the island. I remember as a child being positioned in front of his blackboard. Papa, with chalk in one hand and a pointer in the other, taught me vocabulary, sentence structure, and penmanship the old-fashioned way. His third daughter, my mother, is a former junior high school teacher who now readily tutors adults in the Learning Center at the Brooklyn Public Library. I am a college adjunct who simply enjoys the teaching profession. We remember Papa's lessons well and have put them to excellent use, inspiring and educating others.

Papa came to Brooklyn during a period of mass migration. I found the Schomburg Center for Research in Black Culture a powerful educational resource. Online it presents "In Motion: The African-American Migration Experience." The site notes that distinguished Caribbean migrants came to America during the nineteenth century as skilled craftsmen, scholars, and ministers.[19] Professor Thomas, during my stay at the University of the West Indies at Mona, taught us that from 1900 to 1920 the Caribbean lost a significant number of intellectuals and technically skilled people. This "brain drain" tremendously promoted the growth and development of the United States. It also supported the advancement of Caribbean communities in America. This group of Caribbean immigrants was disproportionately literate, more so than European immigrants of that time and the native-born white population.[20] As we read Papa's letters, we realize he is not only literate, but unquestionably poetic and prudent.

Papa's letters allow us to learn a little about medical history. This area is extremely valuable, because families share many things: genes and chromosomes, communities, food preferences, and daily routines. These similarities can help in understanding, alleviating, and healing past pain and disease. For example, in many of his letters Papa makes mention of Grandma's poor health. In the March 25th letter, he specifically says, "I am constantly praying that you will get rid of the pain in your knee." It just so happens, my mother, my son, and I all have problems with our knees. Medical information and health records of the past provide the research material for the cures of the future. Also, we can study family proclivities and lifestyle choices and perhaps lower the risk of certain future ailments.

Papa's letters reflect his love of words and creativity in using them. They reflect a sense of pride in his penmanship. The utility of these letters are inescapable: it was the most economical and technologically available means in 1913 to communicate with loved ones back in Jamaica. With the advent of the computer and the Internet, technology has changed, possibly endangering the way we are educated, learn to write, communicate, and relate to others. Letter writing as a means of communication and as a permanent historical record of interpersonal relationships must be preserved, studied, and respected, now and in the future.

Several readers of the original four-part series, "Papa's Letters" published by the *Carib News*, sent me congratulatory e-mails. However, many of these communications were mixed with sentiments of sadness and regret for not reaching out to their own grandparents and family members. Some were angry at themselves for their reluctance to learn about their family tree. There is no time for lamentation or feelings of guilt. The time to sit at the feet of the elders is now. Listen open mindedly to their stories, learn from their mistakes, and appreciate their words of wisdom. Bring a pen and pad, a recording device, and a camera to these sessions. If your great-grandparents or grandparents have died, or if family members are in no condition to tell their story, remember that there are several online sites to help with genealogical research. Another point: items like birth certificates, deeds, passports, marriage licenses, military records, church and school records, jewelry, clothing, and even antiques can provide clues to your roots and family tree.

Several years ago, after reading Papa's letters, I began a search for specific unanswered questions. I traveled to Jamaica a few times, made many trips to the Bible, the World Wide Web, the library, census records, homes of relatives, the county clerk, and the Brooklyn Historical Society. During the hunt for pieces of my grandparent's story, I uncovered a wealth of information about the Caribbean, African-Americans, letter writing, the pen pal phenomenon, immigration patterns and the law, new technologies, cultural differences and similarities, historic landmarks, genealogy, and so much more. Though this book is finished, my search and my story are not. I will continue to move fearlessly forward into the twenty-first century. But like Sankofa, the mystical bird of the Akan people of West Africa, I do so while looking back at the past. I have promised the ancestors to live now in the present while pulling the best of who we are into the future with me.

This is not the end

Notes

Chapter I

1. Crown Heights North Association, Inc. *A Short History, The People*. (http://www.crownheightsnorth.com/chn)

2. D. Harman. "Jamaica's Women Rising," *The Christian Monitor*, March 3, 2006, 1–2.

3. Edw. R. C. Earle. "The Mineral Springs of Jamaica, what they are and what they ought to be," *Jamaica Public Health Bulletin*, 1917, 57–70.

4. Dale W. Tomich. *Through the Prism of Slavery; Labor, Capital and World Economy* (Maryland), Lanham: Rowman & Littlefield Publishers, Inc., 2004), 111.

5. Rupert Lewis. "Political Aspects of Garvey's Work in Jamaica 1929–35," *Jamaica Journal: Quarterly of the Institute of Jamaica*, March–June 1973, Volume 7 (1-2): 30.

6. Jim Ingraham. "Labor in Jamaica After Emancipation." Emancipation: The Caribbean Experience (scholar.library. miami.edu/emancipation/Jamaica)

7. Sidney W. Mintz. *Historical Sociology of the Jamaican Church-Founded Free Village System* (The Netherlands: DeWest-Indische Gids, 1958), 48.

8. Goodness and Mercy: A tale of a hundred years by George E. Henderson, Pastor of Brown's Town Baptist Church 1876–1926. Printed by The Gleaner Co., Ltd., Kingston, Jamaica, 1931.

9. Sidney W. Mintz, *Historical Sociology of the Jamaican Church-Founded Free Village System* (The Netherlands: DeWest-Indische Gids, 1958), 49.

10. Brown's Town, Ocho Rios. See (www.visitjamaica.com/attractions/browns-town.aspx)

Chapter II

11. Charles Hirschman. "The Impact of Immigration on American Society: Looking Backward to the Future," Center for Studies in Demography and Ecology and Department of Sociology, University of Washington. This paper was completed while the author was a Bixby Visiting Scholar at the Population Reference Bureau in Washington, D.C., 2001.

12. Bonnie Kavoussi. The Panic of 1907: A Human-Caused Crisis, or a Thunderstorm? (www.fas.harvard.edu/...crisis.../1907/)

13. Jan Rosenberg. Fort Greene, *Cityscape: A Journal of Policy Development and Research,* 1998, Volume 4, No. 2, page 180.

14. Jas Obrecht. Bert Williams & George Walker: The First African-American Superstars. Jas Obrecht Music Archive (http://jasobrecht.com/bert-williams-george-walker-african-america- superstars/), August 17, 2011.

15. Jas Obrecht. Bert Williams & George Walker: The First African-American Superstars. Jas Obrecht Music Archive (http://jasobrecht.com/bert-williams-george-walker-african-america- superstars/) August 17, 2011.

16. The Frogs: organization of African-American theater professionals, 1908 photo by White Studios. (http://www2.si.umich.edu/chico/Harlem/text/frogs.html)

17. *Transportation Times: A publication of the Champlain Valley Transportation Museum,* Winter 2009, page 1.

Chapter V

18. David Barton and Nigel Hall, eds. *Letter Writing as a Social Practice,* Amsterdam/Philadelphia: John Benjamins Publishing, 2000, page 1.

19. In Motion: The African-American Migration Experience. (http:// www.in**motion**aame.org/home.cfm)

20. In Motion: The African-American Migration Experience, Migrations. (http:// www.in**motion**aame.org/home.cfm)

About the Author

"For I am not ashamed of this Good News about Christ. It is the power of God at work, saving everyone who believes ..."

—Romans 1:16

(Your author – Judith C. Lovell)

Judith C. Lovell began writing poetry after a spiritually enlightening educational journey to Africa with legendary Egyptologist Dr. Yosef Ben-Jochannan in 1980. After years of writing inspirational poetry, Cannon Pruitt appointed her Poet-in-Residence at St. Philip's Episcopal Church in Brooklyn. Judith has had numerous articles published. She also enjoys writing enlightening skits and educational short plays. She is the award-winning writer, director, and producer of *"Moore than We Bargained For,"* a riveting two-hour drama about HIV and AIDS and its horrific effects on a Brooklyn family. The play previewed at St. Philip's for World AIDS Day on November 30, 2002 and had a run off-Broadway in 2003. Judith donated part of the show's proceeds to the Balm in Gilead organization and the Brooklyn AIDS Task Force.

For Caribbean History Month in June of 2010, the *Carib News* published *"Papa's Letters."* Its four-part series featured excerpts of her grandfather's exquisite early-twentieth-century love letters. Judith's Jamaican grandfather and grandmother were pen pals, beginning in October 1913. She inherited many of "Papa's" letters. Though she does not have all of his letters or any of her grandmother's letters, she has embarked upon a most interesting and rewarding genealogical project. Judith has expanded the series into this book. She strives to answer the numerous questions readers of the four-part series sent to her through Facebook and email.